Band Names & Other Poems
Peter Davis

Band Names & Other Poems
© 2018 Peter Davis

Published by Bloof Books
PO Box 326
Lambertville NJ 08530
www.bloofbooks.com

Member of CLMP

Bloof Books are printed in the USA by Spencer Printing and Bookmobile. Booksellers, libraries, and other institutions may order direct from us by contacting sales@bloofbooks.com. POD copies are distributed via Ingram, Baker & Taylor, and other wholesalers. Individuals may purchase our books direct from our website, from online retailers such as Amazon.com, or request them from their favorite bookstores.

Please support your local independent bookseller whenever possible.

Cover drawings: Peter Davis, artisnecessary.com
Design & composition: Shanna Compton, shannacompton.com

ISBN-13: 978-0-9965868-7-0
ISBN-10: 0-9965868-7-3

1. American poetry—21st century. 2. Poets, American—21st century.

∞ This paper meets the requirements of ANSI/NISO Z39.48-1992

for Stella

Everywhere the Spring is blazing
With ten thousand shades of blue
And ten thousand colors of red.

—Chu Hsi, "Spring Sun"

Contents

  9 Band Names
15 The Blossoming
16 Ocean Radiator
25 Songs of Our Forefathers
35 On a Given Day
45 Touching Stuff
46 The Issue with Doors
55 That One Circumstance
65 How Each and Every Person Might Respond to Every Situation
79 That One True Religion
82 The Sketchbooks of the Great Artists
91 Small in the Distance
92 Coming Home Again
101 More Compact
102 Foreign Object
111 A Fourth Man
121 Fathers and Daughters
122 The Prettiest Bloom
131 When I Was the Writer
132 Jess's Gesturing
141 The Encumbered Journey
151 The Mind and the Body
152 The Use of Youth
159 Succeeding in America

160	The Dainty Ninjas
169	The Future as We Planned It
177	My Love for You
178	The Winner
185	A Sequence of Movements
186	Best Suited
195	The Lives of Writers
198	Careful of the Panther
205	Nothing Seemed Right
206	The Positions around the Extractor
213	The Diet of Jesse James
214	Changing Directions
221	The Rooster
229	What Matters
233	Acknowledgments
235	About the Author

Band Names

Oath Broker
The We Sells
Sunday Harness
Freak Magnet
Early Comes Later
Fist Trumpet
Birth Bird
Um Crumbs
Huddle Throat
Daggering
Dirt Money
Stoner Ron
Sleek Tick
Pigits
Centers In
Afting
Riddle Violin
Scrubs Not
Florida Florida
Cries Out
Tryst Crimper
Clementine Gut
Grown Known
Upper Clay
Grind Up

Shut Further
Ox Mask
Name Dime
Police on the Stairs
Lips Rip
Roland Thunderclaus
Pathtubs
Early Morning Gross Host
Drink Ghost
Do The
Crisp Collars
Diet Coaxing
Duke Kiss
Torrid Toward
The Dutching
Tramp Tramp Tramp
Tomato Coat
Four Baskets Up
Bumble Rig
Loves Rich Pageant
Culls Grapes
Full Is
Where Evert
Doom TV
Hand Shovel

Goat Silas Goat
Herr Ex
Presumption Gear
Tad's
Gone Blister
Toe Fire
Table Rust
Twinkles What
Westerns
Lip Ship
Le Orphans
Been Mirrors
Block It
Men Into
Other Over
Elephant Isn't
Prom Squealer
Joy Wrote
Cheese Heist
Luck Tumbler
Ifts
Tub Bloat
No Hurt Tweezers
Belly Scares
Dense Leg
Fence Lock
Crow Quiz
Hardened Lamp
Amp Deferred
Aristotle Late

Trans Antler
A Little Bleeding
Sheep Bits
Murder on Lifetime
Lent Quicker
Breads Are
Cleats Don't
Camilla Cosby Can
Carpet Milk
Dire Tiger
The Crimp-Ups
Chick Cape
Belt Chirp
First Big Knife
Loose Shoes
Verse Coastal
Calls 911
Frog Number
Amanda Us
Kitch Kamp
Rolling Thumb
The Bike Swans
Because Stuff
Wolf Basket
Ones Too
Lot Target
Wrist Scars
The Cut Heres
Tooth Sect
Pimple Boss

Osmond Cartwheel
Ohms
Energy Tit
Older Cops
Shark Darts
The Smoke Solos
Tea Rust
Three Window Fire
Lurk Castoff
Fun Dress
Visiting Mrs.
Flip Phones
Cat Exit
Moss Bullet
Money Paint
The Won't Stove
Glass Maze Now
Mass God
Fact Cheetah
The Smell Nice
Kid Bees
Flesh Crisper
Strong Islam
sbobs
Drip Situation
Got Back
Clean Vee
Drink Alisa
The Go Around
Flame Jetski and the Lava
    from Babywood

Babe Card
Meat Pete
The Neck List
Shortened Femur
Waist Finger
Twist Foot
The Book Pilot
Carl Sagan
Gorgeous Florence
The Kept Up
Under Choke
Impressed with Jamie
Tactic Tragic
Dynamite Future
Tall Chagall
Gore Corp
Wax Bat
The Please Tokens
The Speak Brazil
The Fruit Robe
Corded Goodbye and the
    Umbrage of Nozzle
Umbilical Bible
White Under Dirt
Too Much Makeup
Chandler Fascism
No, Nicole! No!
Trump Wall and the
    Mexico Pays
Stored Grommet

Biology Big	Abdominal Apron
Normal Front Lawn	Swollen Leg
Nordic Pink	Braids Galore
Arm Alarm	Pubescent
Bob Dylan Penis	Porta Hottie
Gun Vest	Martini Tooth
The Spit Campaign	Closed Roses
Lunch Toe	Suarez Suarez
Chest Gravy	Her Kids
Darwin Salt	Bush War
Charles in Garbage	Plastic Vice
Foot Braid	Grain Goes Bad
Stale Parade	Soccer Socks
The Stall Haul	The Goop Hue
Drink Scarf	Rush Haters
TV Awareness	Head Leather
Cuss Stake	Dose Over
Dirty Version	The Dodge Pageant
The Backward Had	Badge Howl
Camera Head	The Garfunkel Whores
The Voice Pumpkins	Coked Egg
Norman Throat	Dorsey What
School Roost	Shame Sausage
Diddle Pond	Shortened Foreleg
The Grindnappers	Swine Balloon
Dot Org	Okay Butt
Flag Light	Fluid Palace
Could Not Break Bone	Flute Hurt
Marrow Parade	Worm Heart
George Bruise	Racist Priest

The Communist Throbs
The Hans Clip
Foot Thumb
Extras Welcome
Organized Tamar
Shrink Arm
The Start Hard
Fad Poll
Obviously Phil
Orange Trumpet Orange
Suggestion Bird
Elections Matter
Stiff Stash
Corner Site
Mint Tape
Venom George Talks
Boy Scout Cramp
The Zilch Robot
Zeal Before Honor
Tried Hybrid
Slave Tongue
Punch Hugger
The Gross National
Face Mole
The Cindy Pants
Flesh Flood
Chisel Whiskey
Abuse Mode
Squeals Onward
Host Victim

Fists Laugh Louder
Lank Ants
The Fast Terror
Large Cats
Back Dolly
Half Pie
Red Truce
Verge Climate
The Luke Worms
Tilt Quail
Law Awe
Drain Blanket
Doubting Chomsky
The Hood Venture
Thick Neck
Small C. Christian
Snake Dodgers
The Rapid Q
Vented Jesus
B. B. Cringe
Must Goat
The Jean Empty
Torque Order
Newt Porker
Fly Mustard
The Olive Tigers
The Split Jims
Contusion Truth
Not Yes No
Skin Quiz

Tight Chastise
Bad Visits
Judas Gin
Garfield Power
Shark Chin
Flat Screen TV
Hype Already
Lifting Monica
The New Testament
The Old Testament
Volunteer Army
Private Public
Whack Passion
The Baby Slug
Snake Farm
Snarl Capture
Little Passports
The Vegan League
Church Doesn't
Engine Tomorrow
Queen Without
Dirge Compass
Magnetic Norton
The Of Dream
Labor Saber
The Yardoscope Yards
Ceding It
Mime School
Sweater Mountain
Walling Out Canada

Fuse Roost
Free Italy
Advancements in Technology
Francis Bacon Wrench
Fad Fat
Zealot Dress
A Degree in English
Homo Throat
The Mormons
University Money
Vested in Metal
Lounging by the Pool
The Blossoming
Pool Cute
Smooth Round Cheeks
Communist Sympathy
Al Gore Sword
Swallow Farce
Eye Tricks
Tickets to Abe
The First Murder
Vowel Bowel
The Bowie David
The Hardly Hive
Shrub Club
Traditional Athletes
Salt Bangkok
Big Dangerfield Dig
Dead Astaire

The Blossoming

I was only three feet tall when I shrunk
even further and was two feet tall before
even further I shrunk. At one foot tall
I wasn't tall but I was at least one foot.
When I went to zero I felt as if my hair
was feathered just so—like this wasn't
bad, maybe I could go further. But
at below zero I began feeling lighter,
in a bad way, like a stalk of straw.
As I minimized more I began to feel
reckless, like it didn't matter much
because I was freezing cold, or was I
super hot? It was a tough distinguishing,
like clouds from clouds or business lessons
from bankruptcy. My torso began to glow.
I was already turned
inside out and growing into
a new dimension. As the past
extinguished the growth, the growth
expanded into a new pocket. I felt I was
watching the birth of a universe and
I was, it's just I kept getting smaller still,
till a blossoming fell out the bottom.

Ocean Radiator

"The ocean radiator will not fit in the
cargo hold," said my wife, who was trying
to fit the ocean radiator in the cargo hold.
"It won't fit," she said. "That's what she said,"
I said. My wife said, "No, she said, 'I hope that
the other equipment will work.'" I felt
some relief about this inside, but outwardly
I grew tenser and suggested we work into
the evening. The day was stretching
like the wing of a large bird, sort of fanning
in cloudy sunlight. That's when I said, "Maybe
if we refigure the cargo hold so that its
chin isn't rubbed against the window pane."
My wife first looked confused but then
said, "And move the ears back, so that
the hair can wrap around." It was at moments
like this that I felt most in love. It was
in these precious seconds that love seemed
to mount us like a cape. I felt my arm extending
toward her shoulder, her rounded shoulder,
and heard myself saying, "Baby, now's the
time, it has to be!" She was unbuttoning her
shirt and pulling up her skirt. The ocean radiator
was humming loudly now and the cargo hold
was widening its narrow hips.

Brass Flask
Flat Quest
The Hush Temple
The Back Napping
What We Know Now
Brian Williams in the Booth
The Entire Almonds
Napkin Lap
The Resist Feature
The Mama Right
Light Speed Realized
Roger Fogwar
The Right Mop
First Kite
The Kid Did
Killed Quilt
The Ultra Concern
Hold Your Head Up
Middle School Prom
Gorge Drum
Midwife School
Unfortunate Headlongs
Radio Window
Color Charger
The Rain Perhaps
Drunk Janitor
Stick Poker
Glib Bowties
Wrong Way Ladders
Appropriations

Reeve Haircut
The Mostly Nose
Choke Tundra
Mall Bears
Rad Scholar Rad
Ripped Plumber
Taste Goblins
Let Go of The
Fart Barn
The Middle of the Joke
The I Am Your Fathers
Even the Overcoat
The Trust Government Fund
Brown Leather Coats
Boar Thumb
Ocean Radiator
The Nag
Amazed Crowing
Childhood United
Self Mold
Chrome Opening
Zips Red
Brass Whip
Fencing Elbow
Upright Uncle
Tension Forward
Otherwise No One
Doppler Gaydar
Vicious Inner
Mutt Machine

System Crimson
Vert Turban
The Search for Chin
Junk Planetarium
Prescription Drug Abuse
Doesn't Do Joyce
The Evolution Argument
Cut Cake
What Seemed Like a Plan
Pluto Gut
Dresses for Sex
The Dentist Chisel
Lots of Knives
Screams Kansas City
Brother Bernie
Parking Lot Handjob
Living in Mansions
July Birthday
Wine Nozzle
Breath Before Dishonor
World Literature
Great Artists
Near Single
Clever Hausfrau
A Void
Refugee Tents
Patio Doom
The Feather Bed
Sofa in the Way
Mic Gravity

The Grave Horseshoes
Pleats Beyond Repair
Nape Alert
Puberty Now
Mob Corvette
Inkling Killers
Ocean Coach
The News Mattress
Rag Jinx
Lawns Till Sundown
Okay Your
The Midnight Tank Top
The Small Press
    Conversation
The Organ for Church
Done This
Spit Wisdom
Movies About Obsession
Signature Chicken
Side Effects Include
Nap Bastion
The High Ponytail
The Turn Otters
Not Quite Ian Zeiring
Pistol Kiss
Gringoism
Skin Vault
Close Voting
Pencil Skirt
Temp Fist

The Worst Actors
Cherry Stick
Not Marx
Villains at Home
The Pill Owls
Mink Jinx
Victor History
The Reason Danzig
Hid Lid
Mega Tender
Soft Cosmo
The Gallop Glitch
Reagan's Assassination
Grief Shield
Cop Lobster
Flit Quickly
The Amount of Water
Illegal to Drive Cars
Digs the Wolf
The Jimmie Venders
O. K. Bowling
The In Retrogrades
The Whimper Inn
Charge Murder
Jowl Surge
Proven to Be a Snake
The Leopard Codes
Karma Mom
The Like But
Pimp Son

Wasp Vest
Increases with Of
Orange Run
The Guilt Table
Linda in Robes
The Gas Sister
Opt Apostle
Cat Drizzle
Surprise Fuss
Lifetime Subscription
Poor Hood
Good Food
Eventually Rust
The Rest Atheist
The Had Curve
Fuel for Fusion
Melt Dawn
Parking Garage Roofs
Sabotage Habit
The Sank Whistle
Hidden Thurston
The Christian Olympics
The Let Bull
Horse Storm
Chores for Later
The Glass Has
Brutus Hospital
Vista Tiff
Jenry Hames
Coal Gomez

Gloat Coaster
The Threaten Price
Breast Feather
Oliver Stoner
Org Cluster
Crud from Home
Hemp Skirt
Version of Your Taxes
Flint Water
Trip Quitter
Hitman Visits
Dorsal Phen
Pins on Mexicans
Pig Criminal
The Chase Cage
Kick Visit
Vaster Pastor
Mass Quizzer
Mist Vision
Bald Beagle
The Order from the Governor
Red Scarce
Razor Velvet
Wrench Ticket
Fizz Wick
Mass of Texas
Glove Trouble
Gruff Morton
Word Feeder

Soviet Surplus
Fails to Kill
Propane Access
Stag Stab
Pretending to Die
String Chin
Venison Tension
So Logo
Rope Code
Pope Stools
Tar Win
Simmer Crimper
Goat Hose
Florid Laurie
How Prone
Wire Sniper
Twitch Sit
Puff Milk
The Headache Powder
Room Doom
Dorm Socks
Queen Tut
Blast Disaster
The Cornered Sutton
Gust Trust
Peg Salad
Hurt Summer
Vest Test
Slit Mist
Accuracy in Reporting

Malice Chalice
New Jeans
Cove Victim
Talent Rumor
More So Than Not
The Former Latter
The Dare Square
Smoke Chokehold
Total Hotel
The Body of Mice
The Try Mate Area
Made Coaster
The Shoe Fort
The PEDS
The Begin Skin
Rasp Asp
Jefferson Slaves
Torque Corp
Sunk Vomit
The Stork Moment
Cork Gun
Gimp Cellar
The Book Took
L. Ron L. Ron
Verb Dense
Chore Cola
The Mars Coddle
Gork Taser
Rachel Taste
The Pity Dump

The Ardor Car
University Van
College Lamb
Saying Dormant
Hospital Frown
The Bore Prom
Folded So-So
Red Says Yes
The Doubt Hostel
Cheer Victim
Piss Hiss
The Rodent Note
Trust in Todd
The Mort Version
All Sorts of Horrible
The One Who Found Her
Radio Preacher
Chill Pillar
Vast Ass
The Cast of Annie
Zit Fiddle
The Get Visit
Harnesser
Style Pilot
Skid Bricks
Mist Barn
Vert Ramp
Golly Holiday
Grey Lolita
A Gift Economy

Thin Shin
Gist Mister
Killer Milk
Tart Dart
The Presumptive Nominee
Lots of Dots
Pastor Known Knew
Bad Fracture
Salt Malt
Trim Limbaugh
The Bitty Hamper
Pam Amp
Chase Vacation
Better Guesser
Abraham Pinko
Commie Fag
The Bore Pore
Rudolph Mess
Chaste Scapegoat
A Needle
Task Bastard
Rome Paycheck
The Secret Golden Plates
Ghost Cat
The Parrot Van
Visit Cleveland
Horse Corpse
North Of
The Grapple Apple
Poly Weism

Fat Polly
Dim Pill
Change Ellis
Bone Motor
Vote Pull-Up
Tiger Pile
Shirts N' Skins
Large Howard
The Is Land
Dent Sender
The Artist Formally Known
    as Price
Tupper Dare
Swig Wig
Kip Instant
War Version
The Soon Noose
Sandstorm Algorithm
The Dig Dial
The Joust Out
Wrist Thick
Banning Muslims
Crew Noodle
Crow Most
Seuss Hue
Hi Vile
Not Ton
Delegate Math
Math Salts
Philadelphia Last Night

Panda and a Panda
Eraser Ace
Hands Wide
The Face Day
Gordon Total
The Fold Spleen
Cyst Biscuit
The Window Sinners
Church Effort
The Repair Bible
Vent Center
Youthful Indiscretions
Beer Dust
Samson Poison
Hard Card
The Dew Hurry
Pet Ted
Fact Jackal
Can't Park the Car
The Vroom Parade
Bike Vikings
The Nod Latch
Cave Art
Neck Blister
The Charge Gopher
The Nope Rope
Beneath Ether
Trim Sermon
Grid Victor
The Knot Gotcha

Kitty Soft Paws
Loose Elvi
Kid Brisket
Teal Meal
Urban Papa
Nip Pin
Sent Gravel
Broke Token
Slurry Fur
Den Viagram
Viagra Tag
Sick Quicker
Some Thump
Hum Gum
Bee Keeper
Sleek Alderman
Grump Prophet
Force Junkie
Nanotechnology
The Ramp-Up
Glass Past
A Greater Labor
Snake Vapor
The Hardly Try
The Sit Pit
Penthouse Downer
Caught Tall
Shorter Than Voldemort
If Only If Only
Mostly Death

Chosen Cork
Quick Pickle
The Norbert Clause
Trick Stilts
Bookshelf Collusion
Songs of Our Forefathers
Fun Nun
Noon Moon
Pete's Stake
Video Gimp
Sell Curtains
Wool Alligator
Fiscal Cricket
The Mace Gauge
Mere Winner
The Sky Yikes
Everybody Gets a Trophy
Non Comment
The Sorry Keats
Rolling Marvel
Royal Cord
Your Daughter's Stuffed
    Animals
Morgue Sort
Goes By Purses
Pose Norway
Jug Grudge
El Camino Starlet
Each Visit
Starter Pun

Vaster Synthetics
Kurt Vonnegut Saw Stars
Hinge Heel
Lark Ark
Scrap Holster
Coma Gets Funnier
Crusader Sash
Via Orion
The Deep Wig
White Hit
Rife Wife
The Target Row
Raise Knave
Master Rabbit
July Hand
The Jesus Stash
The Tryst Drummers
Pasty Vase
Naked in Court
Porn Plaza
Golf Bag
Origin Gimp
Utter Mustard
Drip Mitt
Fit Pie
Ivory Cower
The Give Signs
A Version of Yourself
Kafka Raft
The George Vision

Songs of Our Forefathers

My son heard a song and he began
to sing when, without any warning,
I began to sing a different song. My daughter
sang a song, too, while my wife was
deciding which song she'd sing. She
decided and began. Now, with all
four songs going, we could finally hear
the real song, the one that was floating
between the songs being sung. That
song had a trumpet part and I used
my eyes to communicate that to my son.
He used his eyes to communicate a feeling
deep inside of himself that he was different
on the inside than how he appeared on the
outside. My daughter communicated
with her eyes. She seemed to whisper,
"Here is a piano solo." Of course, the real
solo was the one my wife was singing
with her eyes. This eye song had a chorus
and a sadness that lifted from the creases
in her eyelids when she blinked. Now the
song of all our eyes could really be heard.
This song began to seep from my pores
in such a high-pitched manner that only
the dog could hear it. She began wincing

and rubbed her ears on the ground. That
was now the new song and we all heard
it and began using our noses to smell it.
I heard a faint wail in the distance, then
sensed something else, a newer song,
rising from the floorboards, spreading
all around the skin of this little family.

Siege Mentality
Government Drugs
Tin Prison
Jews for Cheetahs
Ordinary Bunker
Sore North
The None Only
Hot Car Sauce
The Monkey Hire
Wire Salad
Guns of Broadway
Moat Boat
The Notable Sofa
Sand Everywhere
Water Saws
Turbine Crime
Towed to Ed
Numb Swans
Fist Tryst
Mountains with Lodges
Perfect German
Con On
The Grab Answer
Meat Free
Known Plaid
Crow Nerd
Drive-Through Knife
The Laugh Parka
Swiss Fish
Standard Pantsuit

Denim Chimp
Sap Gangster
Flat Matisse
Eight Times Before
Just Over the Curb
Club Flub
Distal Pistol
Black Weather Trench Coat
Clay Licorice
Vamps in Cluster
Pajama Stall
Go Ice Pick
Rundown Bump
The Coke Moles
Mercy G-Men
Spring Machine
The Bee Problem
Grendel Party
Foot Stucco
Pinch of Pynchon
Colossal Tonsil
Gum Knuckle
Bridge Piston
The War in Eastern Europe
Stymied Eye
The Drank Blood
Pat Sits Silent
Vince Quickly
Pea Feast
Collab Balboa

Medic Heartthrob
Forensic Twin
Billions of Adams
Museum Temptress
Tussle Rust
Crust Muscle
The Don't Gramophone
Curl Turtle
The Pollute Salute
Giver Gotten
Bushy Skirt
Termite Simple
Fork Gutter
One Dollar Bladder
The Fairer Hex
Pendent Sin
Gender Thinner
Attic Piano
Valid Hat
Pot Rapture
Abortion Doctors
Syringe Dimple
Sauce Boss
Scourge Whistle
Alert Sir
Dirt Puppet
Turd Verdict
Epic Scepter
Fluid Druid
Purge Church

Big Mustache
The Clamp Example
Chin Religion
Disaster Lattice
Sea Pinky
Wail Station
Lice Vice
Planet Hitman
Mars Goblin
The Not Cops
Dove Hustle
Jesus Enema
The Soap Cardinals
Box Store Charity
Alexander Snazz
Rudiment Spent
The Shark Darkness
Wheel Teaser
The Squid Sit
Castrati Attorney
Lace Trombone
The Model Card Game
The Nerve Commercial
Core Bunny
Meanwhile in the Bedroom
The Merit Gurgle
Mass Regicide
The Maybe Cologne
Steer Gearshift
Horns the Size of Daggers

Ripe McCartney
The Grammar Blankets
Camera Standard
Turbans Like Scuba Divers
August August
Pillow Feature
Search Merchant
The Simpson Pension
Bite Idol
The Suck Bullet
The Same Claim
The Gonna Get Born Now
Vase Cave
Dick the Bruiser
Stab Factory
Swept Toward
Drills Involving Rangers
Good Crucifix
Hell Garage
Smitten Swede
1991
The Sport Cancer
A Fool with a Tool
Hydrant Might
The Gets Off Scott Free
Jackson in Your Living
    Room
The Dali Watches
The Company Quest
Q Important and All Ways

Foxes from College
Hinges on Hinges
The Crowd Snorkel
Snark Tot
Wisp Kitten
Dank Bowl
The Chronic Chest Fur
For Blue Jays
Prescription Overdose
Mostly in Sales
Modern Cartilage
Equal Quails
Language Jerusalem
Le Bib
Seven Bacon
Corrupt Muck
Mick Stagger
Rowing in Eden
Operation Sorry
Apologies to the Court
Wall Lawyer
The Grimace Friendship
Emily Folding
Zipper Christmas
Detect Texas
Sophomore Fox
Spiro Agnew in Effigy
Joplin Wimp
The Drones Closing In
Easter Monday

Not A Shield But Not A
The Passport Faction
Angles for Power
Robber Copper
The Unzip
Fair Corsage
High School Art Project
Saw Make Up
Cell Talk
Garden the Target
Pencil Thrift
Sex Cabbage
The Juice Yodel
Fast Food Basement
Desk Fire
Guide Carriage
Fitzgerald Hairdo
Class Frown
Seventh Grade Levi's
Tongue Funnel
The Yarn Drops
Gusto Yawn
The Center Right
Ship Hip
Shag Rack
The Tall Crawl
Nomination Process
Demi Less
Full Mouse
Regular Aspirin

Tan Van
Van Vampire
Chase Cradle
Decent Carmelo
The Banish Gel
Magnifying Ants
Soot Cookie
Past Tense Atlas
The Clue Glue
Fancy Antler
Vert Lamp
Sister Wigwam
The Church Elders
Jazz Casket
Trees for Bridges
Jesus Brochure
The Shop Gripes
Saturn Attic
The Dear Lonny Note
The Very Tail
Moth Dagger
Lest Satan
File Donna
Dino Feather
Ocean Toga
Fig Liquor
Suds Bowl
Fury Fur
Ape Cousin
Lion Beard

The Mega Set
No Button Holster
The Thank Buzzard
The Shawn Mitt
Jelly Toll
Cloven Davis
Lee Harvey Bald
Bird Teeth
Check Bouncer
Das Custard
Alonzo Alarm
The Whip Pidgins
Turn Version
Passion Assassin
Teflon Aussie
Orbit Obit
Pump Tundra
The Backfire Tusk
The Paw Dawn
Loon Sorter
Chief Teeth
Catching Paper Airplanes
Moot Tooth
Mod God
The Lottery Flower
The Below Pogo
The AC Vent
Squirrel Percocet
Sizable Bottle
Robot Saboteurs

Video Game Tantrum
The Checkout Baby
The Demands Of
Harpoon Malpractice
Lawyers Made of Wax
Zebra Priest
The Leper Question
Langston Views
Mammal Gambit
The Jake Sabers
Personal Relationship with
    Cheeses
Cat Data
The Attire Diamond
Grape Pirates
Nape Table
Cork Doorbell
The Pinstripe Photo
This Go-Cart Drama
Bleed Marvin
Fang Banjo
The Torn Acquisition
Head Camp
Bloat Cobra
The Goop Fantastic
Narc Garb
Probable Socks
Zodiac Kitten
The Go-To Pope
Chosen Voltage

Hills Like Cinders
Pork Stogie
Syrup Rupture
Goose Fluent
Waco Tailgate
The Desire Carve
Berlin Temp
Audacity Saddle
Hootenanny Sandals
Fork Gore
Pygmy Insignia
The Nomad Program
Gourd and Savior
Blimp History
Snare Parrot
Crawl Volume
Einstein Ampersand
The Don't Font
The Rib Loom
Spry Spy
See-Thru Cleavage
Chest Message
Dusty Cup
Venison Pension
Bliss Dish
The Simper Limit
Chess Jelly
The Tank Sanction
Roof Foot
Smidge Mister

The Surely Century
Bike Tirade
Bell Bottom Safety
Under Toad
Bum Rump
The Ache Same
Tan Your Hide
Grunt Dump
Brute Tumor
The Tonya Something
Comma Mom
Coma Stallone
Transgender Sump Pump
Ideal Microchip
Chris Farley Sash
Delete Meter
Ringtail Capricorn
Hornet Killer
Dove Landfill
Thin Eyebrows
Needle Orphan
Draft Fear
Tot Ascot
Oslo Hat
Riff Tiff
Crowd Haunch
Instant Plastic
Pink Cheeker
Sodium Podium
The Pea Sheep

The Pint Gym	Porous Orgy
Bald Boss	Cur Net
The Worst Zappa	Oink Horn
Lawn Dart Recall	Dull Sorbet
Yawn Repair	Dot Com
Number Of	Starter Colony
Dorsal Order	The Norway Prognosis
Victim Salon	The Groan Rambo
Wren Criminal	Vicious Tilt
How They Differ	Acceptable Death
The Dollar Girdle	The Moses Rose
The Most Leather Possible	A Hole Punch Motion
Mind Bottle	The Great American Navel
My Foam Cooler	The Humid Cost
Shoe Vista	Inches of Rain
Junk Beds	The Sever Lever
Bunk Heads	Newlywed Plywood
The Capone Bone	Gollywood
The Hump Bunker	Lake Obama
Bread Devil	Hemp Gimlet
The Severe If	Rash Treatments
Service God	Clatter Pattern
Burden Hawk	Girl Money
Near Kisses	Reba Secrets
Scrum Mummy	John the Revelator
Rum Donut	Rapture Cast
Form Bobby	Elbow Intent
Bible Tripe	Tiki Harbor
Orson Corner	The Fame Aim
Lucifer Tooth	Oft

Pluto Feud
Flesh Press
Classic Blunder
Scant Lamp
Hurrah Sauce
Sip Tendon
The Get Visitation
Blast Addict
The Pipe Freeze
The Buzz Wick
A Victory Risk
Jeer Clearance
No Fouls Called
The Picket Wisdom
Record for Later
Her Youngest Son
The Sparkle Dukes
Necktie Violence
Yacht Island
Tornado Facelift
Vomit Golem
The Fish Wilsons
Pivot Foot
Faith Baster
Triple Lockbox
Famous Solider Graves
Pulled Just
The Golf Flog
Chirp Corp
Maze Blanket

Bit Glitch
V for Poinsettia
Prince Fink
On a Given Day
May the First
Stat Gas
Merica Merica
The Colette Suggestion
The Canned Should
The Glad Saddle
Militant Censor
Buddha Hood
The Art Scaffold
The Gift Minister
The Low Quotient
Q Q Q
The Cloud Loudness
Parps
The Power Off
The Conquer Ball
Take Update
The Snifter Resolution
Circus Fun
No How Counsel
Sun Puppy
Iron Oar
Jaw Saw
80,000 Dead
Unity Tent
Didicule

On a Given Day

On a good day, she gardens.
I don't know what she plants,
but she digs in the dirt and gets
an insect bite. She comes in, wiping her
face with a bandanna. I believe there
are ice cubes in her glass. On a good day,
she sorts the bills and talks on the phone.
She is very cheerful when she receives
the mail. She thanks the mailman.
On a good day, she takes her time
at the store, shopping for razors to
shave her legs. She likes her legs.
On a medium day, she has a feeling
when she reads the newspaper
that is a little like envy, but is also
like greatness. There is also a sense
of futility. It is a stinging sensation
and she doesn't like it. On a medium day,
she laughs with her kids. She gets a haircut.
When she is writing poetry, on a medium day,
she is writing with a sense that she is really great.
She thinks to herself, "Fuck, I'm good."
These are delusions of grandeur. She is
self-centered. Her delusions are true. If only
she believed the truth. On a bad day, she's frantic.

She's pissed. She wants the cars to drive
faster. She is not happy with the dirt
inside her head. She imagines removing her
brain with a giant ice-cream scooper. "It is not okay
to be stupid," she says. But on a good day,
she's okay with things. "I'm not stupid,"
she says with a laugh. "Ha, ha, ha,
who's laughing now?" But on a medium day,
she is not eating cookies. On a bad day,
she's got her head in the oven.

Fig Signal
Twig Cigar
Goofy Foot
Soot DJ
Plus Midriff
Dew Alcindor
Gent Vendor
The Light from the Camera
The Body Politic
The Nape Vape
The Suit Fits
True Uses
Chest First
The Dwindle Mint
The Swig Chigger
Zen Gibbler
Dim Twit
2nd Place Robot
Zone Goat
Fresh Dime
Rinse Empire
Bells of Lake Heron
Yes Sir
Stall Category
Some Tunnel
Primary Family
Eco-Sex
Sand Clooney
Dud Horoscope
Free Shirt from Trump

Turnover Hero
Orange Jerk
Smaller Than Crickets
An Ordinary LeBron
Wreck Keeper
The Keep Peep
Novice Chavez
The Yep Pepper
Punish Tent
Peggy Hill Dress Coat
Twelve Short Novels
LPs to Nowhere
Vig Crystal
Fans of Long White Sleeves
Loss Cart
Paper Iglasias
The Harper Lee Follow-Up
Flu Dual
Cassis Play
Das Nasty
Leonardo Plum
26 Hominids
Cold Total
The Knife of the Long
    Nights
Gorbachev Sausage
Carbon Forged in Stars
Dink Calling Card
Heavy Metal Sweatpants
Chub Mother

Most Summit
Cleft Beck
Willie Dixon Line
Good Grouping
Piss Cake
Facecrook
Go Go Kurt
The Hat Bye
View of Houston
Yet Leggy
Pronto Saget
Chug Solo
Outside Jefferson
Cut Brakeline
Shiner Diner
Dork Cloak
The Al Gore
    Presidential Cup
Son Home
Do Nut
Ear Fiscal
But
The Game Plan Going In
The Meg Selector
Sugar Boy
Ghana Verb
Short Lifespan
Eel Surcharge
Ski Milwaukee
Hug Upstairs

Medallion Stallion
Les Mall
Space for Books
Library Pussy
Clit Massage
The Battle of Sunker Pill
Dark Legs
Bruise Flute
Trusting the Physics
Clue Stupid
Frequent Bars
Repent Meter
Forever Feathered Hair
Gets Her Back
Terse Girlfriend
The Tease Bleachers
Lace-Up Vans
Screech Yet
Kneel Demon
Neither But
Your Old Girlfriend's
    Basement
Adding Couch
New Balloon Vapor
A Gee Egg
Rivet Victory
For Elaine Highway
Dread Teddy
Bears in the High School
Posture Suture

Stitched Liver
Makeshift Weapons
A Row of Read Lights
Leather Pastor
Booby Flash
Streetlight Bikes
Think Eden
The Swindle Pimps
Your Full Name
Brisk Whittle
The Suitcase Raise
The Special Horror Lake
The Double Twin
Punctual Tongue
The Stop Clot
Breath Rattle
The Lois Portal
The Drill Bit Scrimmage
Motor Bored
High Rifles
Friends of Romance
The No Total
Sud Deduction
Gel Skeleton
Prom Tantrum
Cain Thankful
Tom Cruise Delusion
Couch Jump
Middle Sid
Christmas Music Suicide

Middle School Slow Dance
Pipe Cleaner
Folding Charity
Loss Apparatus
Atticus Lynch
Sore Judge
Kill Mill
Am Pentagram
Big Trigger
Good Haircut
Wedding Greatness
Very Intense Coach
Stephen Queen
Yep Buddy
Intents & Porpoises
Socialist Voter
Four Score and Seven
A Perfect Amount of Stars
The Annoy Token
Owen Crumples
Straight Left Arm
The Official Hypnotist
Via Toto
The Larger Aprons
Ne' Billy Joel Pas
Close to Ten Minutes
Shot Boa
The Semi Victims
Freedom Isn't Tree
Erstwhile Try

Billie Jean Queen
Cat Cabbage
Nice Mustache
Kiss Detroit
The LGBT Community
Cash Daddies
Hall Lizard
Whence Fidget Lad
The Yo Placate
Christian Sniff
Panty Drawer
No Good Lung
Hats Like Alcatraz
Western Health
Skinned Paws
Cement Shoes
A Version of Robins
Excited About the House
The Sole Incursion
Videos in the 1980s
Warmer Skirt
Pudding Tick
Day Clarence
Gore Template
Junk Planet
Sculpt Skull
A Row of Iron Bars
Caplet Blab
No Notice Hopeful
A Series of Tense Relationships

High O
Struggle Brother
Lie Fife
Certain Kinds of Ponytails
National Dull
Fist Like a Fly
Charted Y
Bad Sir
No Minnow
Minus Minus
Ho Turtle
Steep Hat
Attempt ER
God Shaped Hole
Early Radio
E. E. Somethings
The Hue Cooter
Third Sand Wedge
First Degree Pillow
Thousands of Finches
Sally Loss
Double the Say
Sin Vino
Sour Brown
Dutch Hardware
Bib Terrier
Win Tunnel
Wheel Fix
Smith We Might Continue
Rightway Feldman

Gerald Lord
The Goddamn Quinn
Big Cordless Phone
The Busy Signal Absent
T-Shirts Like Bread
Greeting Salesman
Leather Panther
Vandal Plans
Water Felon
Not Just a Vision
Track Met
Runt Tongue
Org Pharaoh
Mom's Roommate
The Crud Lobby
Glum Rummy
Data Bladder
What You Talking About Willis
Furlough Program
Evades the Snare
The Hand Axe Massacre
School Delay
Oslo Over It
Lord Crybaby
Juice Penny
Pelican Arrow
Hug Bust
Garden Variety
Fade Ray

Bears for Pillows
Paid Vole
The Kind of Episode
Kathy Taking Prisoners
Horns Upstairs
Snitches
Bitch Witch
PJ BJ
The Only Act
Concave Board
Let's Go, Bud!
Choir Practice
Church Girls
Bay of Germs
One of Those Classy Joints
Feather Tin
Tort Happy
Finnish Dog Association
Suspender
Game Perhaps
Georgie Plunder
Stilts for Simplicity
Blonde Quitter
The Hess Mess
Fad Judgment
Practically Dead
Dearth of Cleo
Serrated X
July 1972
Given Stuart

Peso Cottage
Stations of the Crossbow
Wine Tunnel
Lightly Tied
Yellow Grass
The Goal of Camels
Tactful Lad
The Wrath of God
Shatner Farce
The Sort of Coat You
    Button
Future Boots
The Knock Throttle
Blood Kite
Ace Verbatim
Stun Gunther
Labs in France
Frenchy Twist
Gauze Cause
Money Tadpole
Proper Bob
Cass Velcro
Ivy by the Spy
Gross Bloat
Kid Sickle
A Rational Person
The Wages of Nathan
A Great Fish
Breathing Through Your
    Mouth

Skirt Shopping
Hardware Store
Used to Be a Beast
Shot-Up Brother
Me Too
Pictures of Feet
The Skin Cream
College Must
And the Crowd Boos
Sock Rocks
The Handbook Try
Suture Text
Untie Me
The Blame Triangle
Big Old Station Wagon
New Bulb
Banged-Up Car
Tiny Minor
Mike Brady Dumpling
The Dial Telephone
Come on Honey
Frail Men
Obedient Bed
Striped Dress Shirt
Cuff Wink
Shop Class Fingers
Goodnight Creep
Mom's Fault
Do That
Both Judges

Missed It
The Money Whip
Bedridden Wife
Otherwise Mr.
In Favor
Ripped Ticket
The Todd Particle
Personal Butler
Glad Barker
Uh Oh Tissue
The Age We Live In
No Money
Mob Package
Briefcase Snake
Welcome to Asia
European Socialism
Black Sweater
Scotch Baby
Plastered in Paris
The Souls for Sale
Smuggles the Sofa
The Enjoy Envoy
The Greatest Seventh
    Grader
The Spanking Curve
Bell Sour
Afar Starlet
Egypt Swish
Visit Pivot
Getting Colder

Slow Twins
Certain Oaks
Pearl Haggard
Zero Funks
Apartment Doors
Okay Liar
Bleat Whisker
James Bong
Shat Heathens
Tsar Car
Goodn't
The Possibility of Clapping
Possibly Clap
Fuss Maker
Blight Skater
Proud Mama
Pages of Agents
Unfortunate Pun
It Kid
Kent Drinks
Supper Wet
The Wanna Drops
The Edge of Western
Your Magazine Collection
Space Trash
Roof Floor
Buns and Gutter
Arch Enema
Heap Mention
The Ur King

The Finnish
  Disappearing Act
Knievel Breather
Neck Wreck
Mick Wage
Motor Kite
For Satan's Sake
Snake Flavor
A Better House Trap
God Gobs
The Holy Gush
Yes Rosie
Dumb Total
Plus Cousin
The Red Version
Rad Hourglass
Dove Thumbprint
May Not Mayor
Rude Pursuit
Often Bloom
The Dictator Sneer
Michael More Or Less
Film Milk
Whatever O
Dick Very
Chess Fight
The Gunning For
Near Yodel
Chill Visage
Coed Unit

Am Box
Arrow Dare
Boost Op
Po Toledo
The Of Story
Lado Pado
Strike Hugo
Speed Mitten
Old Jesus
The Gnat Pack
Force Yield
Welding School
The Stitch Release
Golden Recover
Dandy Photos
Pea Pods
The Hurry Sleep
Certain Luann
Posters of Motorcycles
The What Cricket
Dawn Hair
Touching Stuff
Stop Circles
Pank Startle
Settle Melt
Wire Springs
The Ha Clot
Prom with Tina
The End Verdict
Color Mode

Touching Stuff

It's your decision, but I wouldn't do it.
I say it all the time: Don't touch stuff.
And when I say it I really mean it.
And I really mean it now, too. You can
touch stuff if you want, but I wouldn't.
It's not that the stuff will hurt you
(at least, not a lot) but that
the stuff will leave a bad mineral taste
in your sleeping schedule. You might
have occasional insomnia or perhaps
over sleep, waking up after
everyone else has eaten lunch. It's
the stuff that makes people like this,
though most don't realize it.
Even as I say this, there's probably
someone thinking, *I don't
think touching stuff is that bad*.
And you're free to think that,
but a reckoning is coming and it
involves the touching of stuff.
You might pretend that the troubles
in your life are of a different variety,
but they are all the same variety,
a certain variety of touching stuff
and thinking that doing so is just fine.
It's a cultural blind spot.

The Issue with Doors

Doors act all nonchalant and doorish
but there's a certain attitude there.
A certain Well-I-could-be-opened-I-could-
be-closed vibe that has an irritating
effect after a bit. I think of this sometimes
when I'm looking at a door. O, the time
I've spent looking at doors! Something
about their hinges make them arrogant,
as if, "Because I am capable of swinging
freely, I am better than you." This issue
with doors has really begun to grind
my bones into a chalky dust. It's something
that can, like, leave me flushed with a
dread, like my spine is a wiggly snake
and I'm shivering with it. Because of all
of this anxiety, I try to avoid thinking about
the issue with doors, try to avoid feeling
shame when I do, try to avoid feeling about
it in anyway. But this is as hard as you can
imagine it might be. All these doors, just
swinging freely on their hinges, their
feathers thrust up high, preening!

Cringe Lesson
Cats Made of Water
Vast Plaza
Block Smarty
Safe Raven
Fresh Deacon
Road Orca
Jet Question
Begin Some
Pablo Capable
The Issue with Doors
Rivet Bigwig
Diverse Purr
The Candy Farts
All Day Tuesday
Paula Jonesesque
War Thurston
Wood Gut
The Winter Can
The Can't Us Faction
The Demo Hearse
Stonewall Onward
Press Viper
Prim Franz
Mo Nettles
All My Gay Friends
Feather Clad I
Square Monthly
Motel Loom
Bled Parsons

Arch Bobby
One More Curtain
Sup Bled
Yow Cower
Yo Big Lies
Coronet Mode
Drowsy Crown
The Nod Because
Weak Official
Star Clad
The Skips In
Blown Call
Faint Mason
Tall Bustle
Sang Hardly
Ping Ending
Store Custard
Un De' Card
Yawnsmith
Dew Lute
Gist Quiz
Shove Bone
Sling Shift
Slates for Later
Trudge Flood
Drag Ladder
Groan Loren
Base Mint
The Plod Plot
At Most

Stuff Meek	Twirl Service
Pill Cheetah	Rid Signal
Sin Pencil	Jar Garbage
Mo Faux	Doubt Sauce
A Real Fox	Pig Stem
The Please Cleave	Everyone of Us Always
Howard Sorta	Rich Beard
Stat Vat	Tongue Bunker
Speck Guess	Locust Hose
Four Tons of Mostly	Deform Stone
Mork Detour	The Gosh Cops
The Din of Fins	The Dental Hygienist
Plum Said	Short Clear Glass
Tens of Thousands	Pat Hology
Famous Stamos	The Bark Spies
No Soap	Blank Jenny
Touch Much	The Studies Inn
Lizard Twit	José Oink
Keep Drifter	Five Inches of Rain
A Smidge of It	Nit Orbit
The Nab Sadness	Ulysses S. Christ
Wow Mom	Big Stagger
Sans Ann	Da Vinci Hombre
Rile Mighty	Rectum Spectrum
Paula Charm	Orwell or Else
Search Urge	Fruit Narc
Measure Legs	Truce Blingsteen
Crane Language	Ray As
Clang Fork	French Doodle
Suede Manger	The Can Mantle

The Cut Vocation
Bless Your Hurts
Station Wagons of the
    Cross
The Urge to Start a Fire
The Teddy Boy Cage
Rigor Fig
Press OK
Lower Hope
Yellow But Also Better
Peace Cheater
Brass Esau
Flesh Pot
Sworn Penny
The Us Blight
Ten Wars
Good Hood
Vinegar Like Wine
Lit Mormons
Upper Cusp
Al Bum
Only Grudges
The Prevent Salts
More Torpedo
Irish Minor
BFF Barf
Flub Sunset
Squid Bitter
Poor Sot
The Empty House Sound

Shin Jelly
Kneecap Bat
The Dead Sea Trolls
Super Thin Watch
The Think Switcher
Hoof Selector
Test Kittens
Vonnegut Scholar
The Shrug Crux
Pork Bullhorn
Radio Chatter
Bus Pews
The Boom Clooney
Neat Scotch
Semi Time Share
The Empty Bottle of
    Tolerance
Solid Dude
So Lid
Gimmick Window
Style Isle
Java Man
Full Knuckle
Fine Diet
Mall Cap
The Mutter Cut
Gin Like Hot Sauce
Party Cowl
Engine Send-Up
Her Curls

The She Fink
Pony Hawk
Fat Adam
H. E. Double Hockey Sticks
The Rot Throttle
The Yolk Notice
Money Clit
Answer Gland
The Guilt Sill
Dock Pattern
Shrimp Stonestreet
The Dummy Pundit
Glove Dangers
Text Kettle
Ugh Bye
Blank Paint
The New Sportage
Gad Gadget
Okie Dope
Get One Free
Satanic Satan
Little Bit of After
The No Souls
Paddler
For Christ's Sake Man
Evolve Squad
Large Blowgun
Pup Little
Marge Garage
Wanda Dawn

Stoke Foe
The Grease Chimney
Far-Off Cough
Situation Sore Throat
Billions of Hardships
Paper View
Supply Mice Economics
Adam Western
Gad Sty
Piles & Piles
Print Journalism
The Stood Future
The Total No Go
The Let Huey
So Long Garment
The Showbiz Quiz
Grass Ladder
Saint Chain
Sober Faces
Swaggart Schwag
Merch Church
Slur Court
Nor Gutter
Lessons in Forgery
Mall Cap
Saddle Factory
The Houston Youth
The Every Others
Both Brothels
Barrels of Toil

The 2nd Commendment
The Carny Harness
The Phased Don't
Knife Light
More Sleeveless
Naked Cake
Slave Cradle
Status Limb
The Jive Mile
Desk Reefer
Pledges of Death
The Kite Vikings
Sister Vickers
The Malign Chimes
The Service Entrance
Coke Head
Berries Like Vital Organs
The Lop Synopsis
Badger Badger
Polly Darton
The Llama Nomad
A Carnation Past
Bottled Slaughter
Charge Hardly
The Clod Whisper
Shaker Drama
Roll Ollie
Tag Savant
The Falcon Con
Tipping the Rum Waiter

Swim Drunks
Prog Rocker
The 70s Nylon
Garter Quack
Slade Clayton
The West Indies Coffee
    Trade
The Kevin Adjustment
Boston in the Ocean
Mommy Fearest
Tide Goes In, Tide Goes Out
The Out Pattern
Seven Tremors
Cleaver Details
The Dish Fags
Coco Robot
Servants with Servants
The Sore Vet
That Kind of Scarf
The Joan Globe
Born Fussy
Claw Matters
The Main Creature
Just a Little Accent
Fur Perfume
Ernst Oust
The Swivel File
Nice Title
The Thump Tummy
The Position Sin

Memories Called Vapor
Tort Deform
Act Static
Row Noble
A Question You Ask
    Yourself
Girl Seether
The Drat Participle
Mock Stalking
Low Floater
Commie Gun
Grade Inflation
The Saddle Grads
Barrage Band
The Emperor Squawk
30 Pieces of Nostalgia
The Double Blind
Chest X-Ray
Face Mason
Space Fillet
Good Shorts
Cleft Nose
Certain Fibs
Bear Toys
Cotton Shadow
Biff Woman
Soft Toss
The Worse Person
Pinch Dentist
The Because Flinch

Huff Princess
Whip It Party
The Gill Slits
Niece Noir
The Yet Fetch
Fluid Pit
Active Liver
The Cried Kids
Rich Skipper
Freaking Whitman
Root Stupid
The Huge Now
The Flood Loot
Ninth Grade Level
The Fork Report
Muddy Mae Huggins
The Crow Flattop
Olympic Fist
Collage College
Miter Paw
Waterloo Bigfoot
Sopping Up Blood
The Chad Fad
Radio Glacier
Stab Gavin
Bon Jovi Wrist
West Bestern
Hamlet Camels
Bliss Dang
The Lovely Company

Close In Counter	22 22
Is Assist	The Sucker Cluster
Ice Bible	A Hinge Perhaps
Frank Einstein	Murder Valet
The New Beatles LP	Jenna What
The Sing Gender	Thig Cricket
Plush Gene	Mortar Beard
The Lesson Goodbye	A Cline Fancy
May Through September	The Same Acclaim
Per Se	Develop Fellow
Best Joseph	Built Weird
Mighty Short	A Vincent That Dances
The Choose Bloopers	Poe Dark
Partial Paint Job	Def Ref
The Slope Fate	Sworn to Mimicry
Gone Yard	The Edgar Allen Night
Target Rich Virus	Horn Etta
Triggers Like Face Dimples	Tim Dinner
Bang Tango	Warden Envy
Favorite Barge	Roll Carson
The Brain Increase	Leg Pagan
The Cambrian Implosion	The Pan Vanish
First Lurker	Claus Vividly
The Blood Chug	Enough of Texas
Foist On	Nuff Buffer
Fonzi Diorama	Gut Check Territory
The Face of Deep Space	These Needs
The Anita Kills	Just Bus
Every Last Coat Rack	Nerve Erstwhile
Post Bedtime	Just Ten Bucks More

Germ Fanfare
Joy Sticklers
Field Barbosa
The Office Dice
Cough Placement
Safe Braid
Average Vat
The Toast Vocation
Solid Cold
The Snakes of India
The Snatch Faster
Sideburn Tourniquet
Zach Bladder
The First Potted Flower
Per Satan
Sashes for Brussels
Kelp Better
Get Bouncy!
Vying for Drama
Various Werewolves
Juggles with Leeches
The Butch Mystery
Jinkies!
Male Sailboat
The Bison Christ
Guile Vice
That One Circumstance
Greedy Newlyweds
The Sad Allow
Intrude Unit

Nine Violence
Carbon Hun
The Sit Audit
Val Tragic
Clean Gut
Presto Brain
Pro-Life Phone Call
Peck Lecture
Live Evil
Swig Tempter
Epic Freud
Floyd Register
Roc Sendoff
The Jill Swish
The Grunt Dumb
Chant Candle
Edge Elect
Yoga Soak
Chance Lantern
Ginsop Bummer
Anchor Thank You
Jaw Talent
Pummel Dunce
Planned Sampson
Mississippi Toddler
Cute Top
Alexander On One Foot
Secret Typist
A Rising Dryness
The Never Ending Laundry

That One Circumstance

That one circumstance was so uncomfortable,
so unexpected and unimagined that I felt
like that circumstance was one
I hadn't ever planned on. Certainly not
at that moment. The way it unfolded went
unpredicted. Perhaps you've experienced this type
of confluence of events. Maybe you can even
relate to being surprised by a circumstance.
I'm often surprised by how similar my life
turns out to be when compared
to those of the people around me. Often times
they, too, seem to know what pain, anger
and happiness are. They seem to have felt
sensations that I can relate with. One time,
in love with a girl, I told a friend. I was shocked
to hear that he, too, was in love with a girl.
I later heard about another friend who was
in love with another friend! I remember thinking,
"Can you believe it? Is this even possible?
Can they really feel what I feel?" I remember
curling up with a blanket to consider these
questions. This is how I feel about the circumstance
alluded to earlier, as if there are questions about it.
That one circumstance, especially that one time,
changed everything. It was a very pivotal circumstance.

Yes, as I examine it further I see there is a light
trapped inside it and I am a jeweler with a tiny
hammer, tapping toward the center, hoping
to crack this rocklike circumstance. I see
now what I couldn't see before, how much
I love you, how strange I think the universe is.

Go Somewhere
Team Captain
So Hugo
Medical Hair
Notebook Champions
Wax Casket
Big Belly Fred
Push Button Mortgage
How You Spell L
The Largest Inventory
    Around
The Haven't
Blake Marriage
Stiff Drunk
Leo Said
First Shave
Doozy of a Sentence
Cotton Plot
Wonder Gum
Past Atrophy
Moping Home
Hey Great
Weak Fee
Heavy Puncture
Just Disappointed
The Parenting Class
Back to Rehab
Sir No Sir
No Cigar
Run Out of Graves

Gun Bust
Dead Betty
Actual Help
Radar Blips
Pool Loop
Freaky Tall
Three Comas
Serious Styles
Cough Better
Get One Free
Cape Placement
Singular M
Pogo Jihad
The Spur Purring
The Honey Done
Leroy Marr
Clearly a Shove
Whack Wreck
The Impact Gag
Yolo Clementine
Leaf Treatise
The Nothing Room
New Beer
Force It
Far Larger
Crummy Monk
Nun Runner
The Putty
Trudging Toward Hope
Glove Uncle

Bunk Head
Bus Bunker
Spearing John Birch
In My Time of Dying
Unanimous Hammer
Amino Acrid
Heart Farm
Red Checkers
Gnash Package
New Jersey Clump
Frank Lloyd Wrong
Far Zan
The Badge Pageant
Fresh What
The Bud Club
Bangs Out
The Leper Test
Pawn Shopper
Apropos O Yea
Little Guy Problems
Talk to the Hand, Yo
Big O Tree
Down Twelve
Be Trey
The Hard Rah Rah
Shucks How
Cleave Beast
Rots in Heaven
Al Overly
Firm Urn

Blitz Tizzy
Sweeps the Hedges
Her New Suitcase
Lounge Downwind
The Y'all Clobber
Rough Semester
Dirge Girdle
Dork Circles
A Case for Punishment
Hell Seldom
Flint Water
All Kinds of Crops
Below Meltdown
Dogs for Allah
Play Kate
While Drilling Oil
New Cartoons
Spit Whip
Gym Skipper
S Labs
Jargon Hard-On
Not Because of Rust
Flannel Tongue
So Go
3rd Slow Glow
Nominal Comma
Gale of Nails
Lumber Numb
House of Blouse
The Chrome Float

Nod Body
Serves Not
The New Cur
Shopping for String
Comfort Fat
Drumming Up Support
The Dollar Menu
Blurts Out
Known Heretic
Lunges at the Trumpet
Fruit Tube
Hot Symptom
Ditch Prism
Belief in Cleavage
Shorn Bundle
Couple of Kids
The Search Averse
Broke Slowpoke
Ann Arbor Job
The Sharp Sections
The Pipe Perhaps
Close Apartment
Dibs Because
Hostile Awhile
Den of Thimbles
Late Okay
Born Yummy
Sort of Lending
Tobias Night
Sleep Villain

Lima Cat
Wolf Tulip
Jars of Arson
Lude User
Hostage Pit
Hell on Eels
Dude Booth
Gimp Kremlin
Church Virgin
Clip Piston
Chet Hat
First Surgeon
Forelimb Hint
Dang Anxious
The Gnostic Gospel
Kidney Problems
Meek Diva
The Leave Neither
New Lester
Knee Pain
Caught Austin
Funk Thunder
Micro Nicety
Fusion Lute
Tiger Lily
Clutter Blindness
The Youngest One in Curls
Secret Crease
Tomorrow at Three
Plush Nader

Vague Front Door
The Is Mission
Meant Well Bob
A Note Under the Door
Purr Gator
Swell Virgo
The Q Source
Guilt Guild
No Half Dollar
Gregor's Sister
O Gee
Summer Dump
Proto Urge
Mostly Because
The Failure of Prohibition
Tulsa Node
Baloney Baloney
Do Brutes
The Juniper Plan
Backs Tab
The November Criminals
Shoot Anyway
The Tact Act
Recent Seattle
The Up Collar
My Fifteenth Birthday
Tension Inch
Deer Head Corset
Same Error
On Our Own

Dawn Comet
The Donation Goal
TV Thinner
Goat Mower
Split Ditto
Tabernacle Cattle
Clapton Hand Grenade
Furry Norris
Government Tiptoe
Slander Fund
Wish Blister
The Modern Day Space
   Program
Ninja Bat Ass
The Walsh Family
The Increase Care Plan
Fat Skull
Nam Airmen
Control Bruise
Boo Politics
Tell Me Nothing
White Track Suit
Opened Bell
Fake Applause
Standing O
Sucker Phase
Hardwire Speech
Birds in Slow Motion
Found Bone
Really Bad Acting

Rockslide Ruler
Mystic Cop
Darn It Farm
Mob Cop
Two Times Faster
Work Toward the Prairie
Belt Cuckold
Clay Faces
The Dot Bravo
The Same One from
    the Dream
Panic News Crew
The You're Gonna Die
    Cough
False Posit
A Number of Guns
Mangle Hand
Pup Trub
Del Led Del
Zonk Gog
Crossbow Apples
No Words
VP Steeple
Severe Period
Kills for Leisure
Chain Link Scribble
Nuck Chorris
The Be Stoic
Bee Shins
Lex Texture

Placebo Veto
The Grit Twig
Shrug Lugar
Paranormal Now
Plaza Lad
Forfeit Dumpling
Old Man Wheelchair
Fret Daddy
Oxygen Hank
Super Tiny Pills
Dirt Flag
Sugar Bleed
Tummy Pain
Ghoul Till
Warning Shits
Heal Ticket
Vibe Killer
Please Don't
One Money Gumption
Shirt Jerker
The Fourth Font
Dive Right
Orth O. Dox Y'all
Divide the World
Gutted Horse
Discredit the Witness
Been Shanklin
Old Giant Phones
Dial Drone
Fracture Shop

The Cameron Ministry	Axe Guy
Speak Hebrew	Rule of Thump
Bullets That Miss	Be Quiet
Solider Smolder	Wooden Sailors
God Triage	The Mile Digress
Deathbed Recession	Swimming the Channel
The Bad Guy Patches	Gruff Lotion
Exit Headdress	The What Good Hands
Super Antichrister	Ginger Shiver
Nine Messiahs	The Tallest Yacht
Skimpy Bone	Teacher's Bet
The You Pray	Con Fection
Glob Locket	Lace Phase
Hi Cheeks	Rope Basket
Brett Fretter	Deny Fredo
No Dave	1. 2. 3ish
Poor Brad Pitt	Animals Worth Cuddling
Unopened Throne	Clue Touché
The Feeds Neatly	Library Sex
Barefoot Children	Lie Lye Lie
Ponytail Handle	Proof Glut
Yikes Bikini	Family Nam
The Really Memo	Futile Pill
Sideburn Domination	The Oft Toss
A Half Glass of Vodka	The Clobber Squat
Lout Coffin	Lotus Nuzzle
Heavy Instrument	Poe Try
Row Boast	Blot Dodger
Banker Fangs	The Loud Clack
Tobacco Pie	Broke Moat

Top Pot
That Sort of Bread
Model Coddle
Drinks Made with Whiskey
Gravy Chaser
The Trouble Bean
Brutal Cupid
Long Black Tube
Everywhere Camera
Wasn't Raised Right
Con Tester
To Use More Zs
Only Hobknob
Diff Dent
Kid Perfect Smile
Torn ACL
Wheel Career
Rare Terrible
The Can't Be Friends
Cancer Likely
Now Won
Isn't Kissing
Orp
Crane Kick Continuum
Avian Flute
Tokyo Dance Job
Wind Din
The Daniel LaRusso Walk
Sauna Bad Guy
Sunken Rotary

Little Trees
King Lame's Version
Bubbles in the Bathtub
The Training Montage
VHS VCR
Fun Sins
All of the Evidence
Cheetah Beat
Too Soon Puma
Grocery Tart
Paper Window
Did Business
Building the Biggest Room
The Bus Birds
Everyone at Risk
Street Hawkings
The Yearlong Menu
An Emma Watson Matter
Prior Gemstones
Workers Named Niles
The Sole Lou
Total Chums
At It Badly
The Strength of Demons
The Rock Last
Lasso Dope
Nowhere Till Nightfall
Drowning the World
Frogs Everywhere
Breast Milk Bone

Ends in a Whisper
A Million Minutes
Bull Notice
Dirt Thunder
Clip Nixon
Thicket Wince
Easy Deuce
Plan Jammer
Dead Wedding
The Had It
Sin Winner
Your Poor Niece
French Cigarettes
Bunch of Onions
Upon Tom
How Each and Every
   Person Might
   Respond to Every
   Situation
Measure Neck
Able to Drive
John F. Frenemy
Any Means
Neat Cougar
Hurry Hearse
The Christ Jesus Fishery
Sap Bladder
Real Bleary
Needle in a Paycheck
Classic Ass

Foreskin Options
Crappy Rapture
The Closet Wasp
Funk Tundra
Noon Juice
A Boost Room
Cut Grass
Lick Slick
Abasement Parade
Milk Figure
The Functionary
Doling Out Abortions
Moose Tutelage
Cheney Lies
A Future of Robots
Devil Sweater
The Stitch Pickup
My Telegram
The Candor Condor
The Rouge Collude
Filthy Wick
Planned Annie
Bomb Dogs
Regular Throttle
Knack Swears
Club Rumormill
The Of-Course Statement
Flake Takers
Unpaid Chores
Stun Florid

How Each and Every Person Might Respond to Every Situation

One person has been to the moon while
another person visits a beach or some other
destination. One person enjoys rollerblading
but another person is a dairy farmer. I've heard
of it. Some people own and maintain
different types of boats and docks.
There are whole committees of
people who consider boating policies.
A person might have a dog or a cat.
A person might enjoy knitting or bowling.
In other parts of the world, people
enjoy local traditions like eating
at a certain restaurant at a certain time
of the year or singing a certain song
at a certain event or whatever.
One person wears a headband,
another person is a firefighter.
There are people in this world
who wear makeup and others
who wear bright orange slacks.
I once heard of a person being rushed
to a hospital. There was another
time I heard about a person
who shopped at a local market.
People sometimes develop interesting

ideas and sometimes those ideas
become inventions that other people
(those close in proximity, or not)
use to the betterment of their lifestyles.
Sometimes a person acts in a way
that is selfish or cruel, but that same
person can also be wise and kind.
I've heard of people who have very
complicated personalities.
There was a person, for instance,
who felt one way about something
(and really felt strongly about it)
but, at the very same time, felt an
entirely different way, as well. It's like
sometimes people aren't consistent
or transparent in their motivations.
Some people work as teachers for a living
but other people have different occupations.
A person can make brick walls for a living
or manage different kinds of mutual funds
for a third party. There are people who
are landscapers and there are people who
drive trucks for a living. There are people
who really like a certain thing, and other
people who really don't have feelings for
that thing, one way or the other. People can
be totally apathetic, but they can also

be vindictive and unreasonable. Some people
are put in rooms they can't leave because
other people have decided, "That person is too
unreasonable to let out of this room lest
that person violate the sanctity
of personal liberty." Some people care
about this sort of issue, others care about
other issues. Some people say, "I don't really
have feelings about these issues, either one
way or the other." People steer interesting
transportation devices like skateboards, bikes,
rickshaws, hang gliders, wheelchairs and
go-carts. Even as you read this, the odds are
very good that some person, somewhere in the world,
is steering a transportation device right now. While others,
of course, are not. People stand in circles sometimes
and sometimes people stand in rows. People can
also sit in circles or rows. People sometimes
form long lines and other times they huddle
very closely together for warmth. Some people
have enough money to live comfortably, while
other people struggle. Some people don't eat
very much food or have a shelter to sleep in. Other
people aren't like this though. Some of them have
elaborate shelters and food prepared by
good-looking and well-mannered chefs. A person
might like one kind of sandwich, another person

might like to eat soup or bread! One person
goes to school for an education, another person
doesn't go to school for some unrelated reason.
It's interesting, but there are many variations.
For instance, one person is tall and wide while another
person has a slighter frame, a more petite build.
A person might prefer one 'like' over another 'like.'
Like, "I like to listen to earthworms more than Mozart." Or,
"I like this sort of pillow more than that sort of pillow."
One person goes to work every day, another
person has a more flexible schedule and can take
a Monday off to watch a basketball game. For another
person, that kind of flexibility might be hard to
comprehend. Some people have more imagination
than some other people. One person can have a talent
in a certain area, while another person can have
a different talent, in a different area! A person likes
rain. A person doesn't like rain. A person likes
contemporary American art. A person doesn't like
contemporary American art. One guy (over in that
portion of the country) does one thing, but this other
guy (over in this other portion of the country) does
almost the exact opposite. One person loves her children,
one person doesn't love her children. Some people
have a really hard time with empathy, but others
are very good at gymnastics. One person does math,
another person grows a mustache. A person's parents

might be dead or alive and a person might have
any number of feelings about his heritage.
A woman enjoys scrapbooking, while another woman
is a star tennis champion. A person can look for
a long time at a sunset, or a landscape, or a tree,
or a person can not consider those things at all.
You get one person who likes looking and another
person who doesn't like looking so much. What
can you do? A person buys a certain type of breakfast
cereal, but not everybody buys the exact same cereal.
Some buy one brand of toothpaste, other people
invest their money in antique beads! There are people
who like toy trains so much that they have little
toy train conventions where they share in their
collective enjoyment. But toy trains aren't everyone's
chief interest. A person might have a number
of different of jobs in their lifetime or they could
never have a job, it just depends. Predicting what
a person might do is really hard without knowing
the person and what circumstance that person
is in, but sometimes a person can be somewhat
predictable. Say, a person might drive the same way
to work every day or they might always apply
a certain amount of butter to their bread, in a certain
fashion, say, with a fork or the back of a spoon. Lots
of people do similar tasks but accomplish them
by varying methods. So there's not just one way

to brush your hair or tie your shoe or enjoy
ice cream. Lots of people have opinions about
how best to do something, but most agree
that there is more than one way for something
to be done. A person might put wallpaper
up in one bathroom but decide to paint
the walls of another bathroom. This sort
of thing happens all the time. Another person
uses one type of air freshener in one room
but in another room—no air freshener at all! And
this idea applies to more than just air freshener.
There are many, many ways to organize
furniture in a basement and people experiment
with those possibilities. One person doesn't even
put an end table in the basement but another
person can't fathom doing something similar.
It all just depends. It just kind of depends
on the person and what feels right or wrong
to them. There can be a lot of factors involved.
It just depends because there are a lot
of variations possible and it's hard to know
exactly how each and every person might respond
or react to any and every situation.

Zoom Zapruda
Five Nightly
Right Kind of Cactus
Geez Police
Slung Tugboat
Hit Dynamite
Expo Does
Cloak Runt
Snipe Viking
Plunge Go Right
Swank DNA
Forge Stunner
Voltaire Salt
Anger Payout
Metal Cassette
Yep Owen
Paid Grape
Seer Sucker Bunker
Lead Keg
Head in the Freakish
   Atlantic
Lony Stonesome
Fork Eyes
Spin Toward the Kingdom
Pissed VP
The Whole Thigh
Vials of Liverpool
The Cages Crawl
Ala Renée
Man Abraham

Pretend Shrink
So Much Bread
Little Spots of Land
Jick Magger
Lester Fester
Rowing vs. Wading
Infant Mortality
Bark! Bark! Bark!
The Chagrin Template
Judge Latham
Panda Obama
Lag Tut
Borkian Goatee
Kilt Too Brittle
Saturday Francophile
Sans Widely
Pounce Lounge
Dapper Whatever
Land Slid
More Witch
Lousy Doom
Cell Phonies
June Through August
The Goddamned Bottle
Peck Winston
Finch City
Cave Babies
The Nag Patent
Streetlight Nightlight
Drunk Missionaries

Fern Burden
The Clear Yips
Fur Liner
Iffy Gift
Mud Crow
Given Premise
Drill Filter
Brink of Gender
Half Calf
Leak Defense
Done Plummet
Select Beggar
Armored Trick
Bullet Roof
Robbed by Magi
While Lying
Vice Guide
Subtle Brother
The Wed Betters
Nap Handclap
Trick Pig
El Swelter
Vegan Murder
Ava Wave
Pester Reb
Grand Adulthood
The Lunch Mables
The Worse Person
Curbs for Skating
Clearly Def

Mo Appens
The Promise Nonsense
Closing Doors That Open
Credit to Ginger
The Grease Bleed
Needlenose Liars
Gas Action
Norms in Waco
Grim Ethan
Church of the Poison Mind
Get Bleak
Tubs of Murky Water
Patter At
Slang Angie
Runway Colors
Snooze Neptune
Sappy Grad
Bled Mimic
Trips to Lake Michigan
Friendly Jeans
Swan Overtime
Heed Ed
Point Razz
Shoulder Chips
Buried Opal
Torch Porch
Ester Pet
Zero Feet
Somewhat Gimme
That Kind of Deceit

Black Metal Telegraph
Morph Org
Elbow Lump
Rome Plaything
Bad Movie Marathon
Seven Bones
The Hammock District
Eight Story Book
The Bloat Pope
The Ism Collision
No Kind of Taxidermist
Grief Seizure
The Prolonged Tumble
Blast Lava
Sugar Basin
Subway Doors
The Fisticuff Button
Red the Color of Alcatraz
Position Twist
Glass Tassel
Unwanted Hair
Super Pubes
Clever Sheriff
Fur Hat After
Narrow Fairly
The Strung Up
Snow Across Alaska
Bloody Dog Leg
Jumper Cable Face Rub
Sweet Greenhouse

Swan Stuart Swan
Solid Silver Teeth
Hex Leather
Hampire
Wax Toggle
What They Did to Gus
Okay Vocation
Ego a Go-Go
Suffer Mustard
Beloved Dud
Brute Tuba
Pubic Duty
Fuse Uses
Bluster God
Duluth Boot
We Agree
Axe Swing Set
Neck Chopper
The Headless Tally
Golly Darton
The Acquittal Mill
Blood Beard
Mousetrap Attic
All Eyes Look Up
Memo to Reno
Sledge Bell Tower
Blip Piston
The Above Deletion
Play Ache
The Behind Tyrant

Tame Zander
Phillip the Circumstance
Sham Campus
Fly Gadgets
Smash Head Footprint
Crystal Vital
Grace Hasteners
Safe Crayfish
Wood Balloons
Pill Age Vacation
Scar Garden
Benedict Give
Somewhat Stock
Rupture Cupboard
Nor Corgi
Lost Rat
Brass Lasso
Foist Boy
Galoot Fusion
Mania Saint
Your Local Listings
Schism Chris
Alleged Dietitian
Bliz Zardo
Rod Codger
Blur Rosebud
Dig Kipper
Proud Doubter
Shiny Truckers
Him Blender

Bench of Skulls
Cater Satan
Radio Oopsy
Juice Foolery
Best Lion Forward
Victory Pal
Head Platter
Jade Facelift
Beg Test
The Base 2,000
The Ought to Snap Faster
Fade Delta
Good Terms
The Ain't Exit
The Twin Increase
Glory Thurman
The We Not
Neon Free
Grid Piddle
Sworn T's
The Long Black Cloaks
Snip Bitter
Cattle Lad
Win Blemish
Punk Bunk
The Larger Cistern
Scabs in Plaster
Plod Matter
Clank Melville
Grey Pants

Stag Axis
Torment Window
Certain Magazine Features
Flame Rainbow
Guest Legroom
Signet Getter
Cloven Hotel
Gown Tower
Cages Full of Giant Teeth
Marginal Cough
Smoocher Tool
Slack Chaperon
We Sheep We
Bun Lummox
The Kitty Cam
Nebula Felon
Quark Garage
Turtleneck Summer
Swap Caviar
Went Goliath
Grump Wardrobe
Buzzle
Voo Don't
Bunny Collector
Slimmer Shin
Forgone Roost
Clint Eons
Steep Prestige
Tank Top Winter
The Revisit Bitch

The Bike with Hand Brakes
Loot Tool
At Most Jason
The Plus-Fours
Gab Crinkler
Heavy Caught
Serf Kettle
Soft Drawbridge
Spur Lever
Inch Work
Cruise Lute
Freddie Pelvis
Went Wood
Ferns for Sanders
Weeps for Odd
Holster Show
Right Hackett
The Kim Penchant
Glove Total
Laid Vacation
Real Nudie Suit
Point of Contention
Function OK
Sledge Correction
In Between Dimes
Pledged to Voldemort
New Dentures
Fled West
Crutch Tricks
Landscape Nanny

Wait Tracer
The Wreck Elect
Snide Pie
Ms. President
One Tamar
Trill Listener
Big Thick
They All Jump
Writers Named
　　Hemmingway
Little Tiny Flags
Half Lass
Dinky Pink
Finding Midge
Hank's Wife
Coma Splice
Devicer
Puncture Comma
Doddering Todd
Mainstream Dixie
Pinko Fiction
Gin Swindle
Hot Bod
Stone Cold Ox
Stain Lesser
Black Rice
Draft Fear
Barn Garter
Dumb Mutiny
Stern Kerning

Bleach Easter
Said Better Dead
Keys Named Lucifer
The Get Rid
Solid Dig
Frontal Lawn
Comfort Foot
Inform Junkie
The Carve Thinner
Mudnight
Lewis Twist
Blur Steps
Fun Shotgun
The And Scandal
Saves David
Nag Prattle
Houston Lucifer
Rumor Lude
Fed Larva
Beg Feather
Twinge Sender
Lord Cord
Lucky Plunk
Clearly Festival
Vacation Hank
Verb Détente
All Around My Hometown
Gun Club Autopsy
Your Brain on Drugs
Glint Gimmick

Hemlock Heartthrob
Drunk Ghost
Red Credit
Fork Rift
Gnaw Bonnet
The Instead Bed
Bad Maggots
The Clank Industry
The Nude Pool
Cake Sham
Beggar Section
Hi Noon
Deacon Funk
In Bed with the Mob
Swan Combat
Dark Pink Lens
Replaces with Anton
Alistair Heave
Short Forelimb
Tidy Jinx
Bored Cairo
11 O'clock Staid
The Domestic Beers
The Swinging Fences
Photoshop Boss
Giga Bitten
Jenna Jamison of Man
Scank Chandelier
Fat Cops Running
The Clay Otters

Other Arrows
Feather Dusters
Etta Vendetta
The Paper of Record
Tool Afternoon
The Vamp Amp
The Other Duggars
Neo Tails
Vestigial Gill
Deep Wimp
The New Job
Sister Bees
Man Vorrison
Leg Cork
Good Mutt
Saluting Liz
Chess Pagan
Binging on Fire
Letter from School
The Blessed Roger
Gorging on Crowbars
Florid Punch
Mod Rim
The Good Tip
Cute Doctor
Vail Thin
The Learn Randy
Cat Mascot
Glass Bed
Mutually Assured Distraction

Dumb Up
Uffer
Level Pal
Snow Named Teresa
Dope Slow Poke
Liar Liar
Fate Grenade
Probable Lot
Good Cushion
Ever Better
Apple Mouth
Stem Rivet
Cooler of Ice
Becoming Corset
The Best Vices
That One True Religion
Ten Members
Dorm Crunch
The Doom Barrette
Yet Nettles
Goats & Cattle
Clutch Bucket
Grand Pinto
Urn Gum
Extra Barefoot
The Timer Button
Girl Bunny
Bismark Spear
Sweet Gremlin
Son Fungus

Mick Tickles
Metal Auger
Crimp Winter
The Swish Till
Lavender Fat
In Place of Possums
Black Cheeks
Bonus Phone
Top Off
Next Hex
Flex Correction
Notice the Taser
The Bet Lecture
Orange Spats
The Cuff Minks
Karate Slobs
Vice Python
The Clever Let Down
The No-Good Neighbors
Burlap Sheets
Movies Starring Wrestlers
The Festering Rest
Valid Snazz
Grim Wife
Vials of Mojo
The Cardboard
Win Dow
White Loafers
Willing Switch
Horse Label

That One True Religion

One trouble with one religion is this:
it only wants to date the pretty girls
and boys. This religion tends to say, "Yes,
I'll go to the prom with you, but you better
look good when we're having sex."
Religions often have mixed-up feelings about
ornaments and ornamentation. So much so
that one religion might take another
religion to court and sue him for leaving
his porch light on for all eternity. This sort
of religion is personified as a male, but
a female religion might say, "You had
either better, or better not, touch my
waist gently." Religions have a sort of oyster
inside of them that forms because of
agitation. This oyster inside has nothing
inside. But some religions might want to
steal ripe oranges from some grove where
the oranges grow in clumps, like celebrity
deaths. One religion believes in one thing,
but a different religion doesn't because
that religion believes another thing.
Some religions make things out to be, like,
"Look, the world is easy here, this life is
nice," but other religions say, "No, this life
is awful, look at the maggot-filled world."

"But there is another world over there,"
says one religion. "Yeah?" says another, "Well
there is a world over *there*, too." "Yeah?"
says yet another religion, "Which world
are you referring to? The world of possible
awful or the awful of possible worlds?"
A bookish sort, in a robe, rubs his glass eye
and says, "I'm afraid God has said something
quite contrary to that." But, there is a woman
who can overhear this from the hall
and she says, "That bookish sort is a real
misguided fellow." She can tell you a story
involving a clam and the waters of the earth
being poured into a bean stew from a cloud
who reigns above with an iron spoon.
Once she gets going with the iron spoon
a frog leaps from her mouth and this frog
croaks a new word, which, in turn, spits
out a new frog. A man in a dress coat
and wearing a silver hat says, "That new
frog says something profound to me. It is as
if that new frog sings a new word." At which
point the frog sings a new word and everyone
listens, the whole room goes quiet, the only
things moving are the feet of the children
in the back row. One of the children waits
to become a man named Ramos who will
lead the ten tribes of Ten Tribeland to a new

place that will be dubbed the New Tenfold
Tribeland. In this city great altars will be
erected to new leaders, those with names
like Jack, Sammy and Keith. One religion
prefers Keith to Sammy according to many
passages in their rolled scriptures. Another
religion just doesn't trust life or death
or Keith. This religion (and its religious kin)
prefer waiting for rain to know if the prayers
for the dead have been effaced. Another religion,
one with an animal coat and gold shield, really
goes further than most in how it denounces
fog and lets a new sauce, a sort of thickened air,
into the bloodstream. But a friend of a friend
knows a friend who believes in a religion that
lets him gyrate wildly in little freak-outs, all
the while whispering the names of bands.
It all gets a little baffling. You start to think
you've seen a shadow but you've really
only seen the shade of an overhead lamp. This
sort of frequent misunderstanding becomes
more juicy in the wee hours of the morning.
On spring weekends, when everyone is eyeing
some new method of thinking, a new religion
blooms and this one is called a different name
than all of the religions that have come before.
That's how you know it's new.

The Sketchbooks of the Great Artists

There are figures and objects in these
sketchbooks, some discernible and some less so.
Look, there! That appears to be a leg.
Look, there! That looks like a windmill.
There can appear to be overlapping figures
sometimes, like cave paintings on top
of other cave paintings. This one great artist
liked to draw animals like cats and horses.
Another great artist liked to draw fruits
and vegetables. Another draws trees, another
clouds, and yet another the veins in a cadaver.
One can see a wide variety of drawings in
the sketchbooks of great artists. There was
one great artist who drew his children as
little squirrels and his wife as a mouse wearing
a peanut shell for a helmet and riding a tiny
mouse bike. This artist drew a starfish with
a smiley face on it. This great artist also drew
other scenes of domestic life. This artist
had a family, it seems, and a sketchbook.
I bet he enjoyed being with his family. And
I bet they enjoyed being with a great artist.

Flower Print Shirts
Lust Pellets
Open Robe
Sham Planets
Shade Monkey
Clump Thunko
Sheep Fizz
Pleather Shed
Sunsetter
Youthful Ward
Shaft Lacquer
Short Panther
Bone Tiller
Mantra Spark
KO Spork
Huge Mice
Crunchy Bangs
Pills You Name
Starter Pit
Stunt Ladies
TV Fireball
Resident Blows
Crib Sheet
Gas Sag
Forlorn Shatner
Man Pants
Scald Pattern
July Rooftop
Legs Marmalade
A Rainbow Spy

Congeal History
Severed Achilles
Spindle Wings
Cheap Black
The Sketchbooks of the Great Artists
The Hostage Shortlist
Cleats of Fiction
One Tenth Eel
Potion Intel
Lid Tidbit
Kid Sinkhole
Garbo Look
Broke Moat
The Move Cricket
Cat Slop
Tall Quit
Slinking Through Amsterdam
Prog Economy
Bad Owl
The Cad Office
Piles of Cash
Bird High
Plum Bump
The Handmade Hello
The Richard Blisters
No Room for Green
Cash Flow Blow Torch
The Last Day of School

Friday Thief
Loon Starter
Skimpy Holster
Shit Gun
Fling Somewhat
Nudge Curfew
A Few Feet Forward
Derby Soot
Lobster Pop Star
The Long Slow Details
Lower Foot
P Sea P
Nun Kitty
Glass Bedpost
The Strain At
Strong Ropes
Snow Free
Mere Peach
Raw Onion
The Stan Dards
The Former Professional Athletes
Stomach Lodge
Land Bedtime
Suffer Love
Clink of Skin
Shades of Yellow
Spike Kite
Worse Church
People Agreeing

Metal Tongue
Bummer Cur
Plastic Tadpole
Hatch Goodbye
The Dormant Slide
Air Conditioners
Nice Lifetime
The Smear Campaign
Teenage Victim
Mercury Pie
Laser Purple Sky
Few Needs
Target Sped
New Comb
Daring Parents
Table Knot
Verge Clergy
Color Snob
Gwen Key
Goes Bump
The Clouseau Era
Name Viking
Mustache Gadget
Gas Lasso
Latent Band-Aid
Lamb Plan
Drunk Prof
Trouble You Yet
Glis Ten
Yank Cave

Trial by Fury
No Remote
Lazy Plaza
Place Molder
Begin Flincher
French Trees
Spare Gel
Chariot Bear Hug
The Stop Gesture
Brother Sweat
Keen Skip
The Measuring
Sorta Octopus
Meal Tweezers
Planet Square Knot
The Fetus Week
Hats for Life
The Slim Vendors
Channel And
Pairs of Shoes
Bly Rum
Leather Chairs
Something Potty
C'est Bliss
The Silk Trade
Pee L
Next Day Drone
Glam Pistol
No Where Jeans
Lisp Getter

Table Rake
Belly Lesson
Two Works
Plastic Tie
Slant Plans
Assembly Kick
Wince Timid
Tea Cozy
The Doily Patrol
Fort Snuck
The Ideal Climate
Cry with You
Slumber Kitchen
Kill Wit
Spring Photo
Potato Satan
Fickle Kin
Beat Teenager
Mate Ratio
Skeleton Welt
Gel Leg
Aim Tournament
Camp Puma
The It Limit
The Sore Portion
Basement Crud
The Bereft Guess
Slings and Sparrows
Sham Ambulance
Liable Ants

The Whittle Fix	Kings in Search
Glam Lamb	Small Movement
Pod Lock	The Plus Hustle
Derby Punts	Yum Register
The Bid Apparatus	Side Water
Face Griffin	The Correct Greg
Feckless Bet	Still Dead
Awe Flowers	The Education Lobby
Timid Rex	Forced Game
Slug Penchant	Window Seat
Hip Promise	The List Enough
The Guilt Till	Lobb Yist
Micro Crow	Oracle Club
The Bring Imp	Bowtie Afterlife
Pure Jury	Shred Letter
Purple Urge	Led Weary
The Collide Side	Decline Knot
Skin Rabbits	Cur Rent
Pest Tube	Celeb Bed
Pleasant Etch	Stoner Tool
The Give Ups	Dug Pond
Sea Leaves	Wolf Eggs
Trick Knee	Smoke Tut
Ain't Percent	Spectacular Fast
Chance Kiss	Track Star
Nod Pod	Animal Cinema
Mark Tween	Able Squirt
Bit Dense	Turn Pummel
Woe Total	Butt Humble
War Bounce	Stick Splints

Colt Muster
Charge Chamber
Bite Crisis
New Toother
The Dick Boost
Hoof Chopper
Antler Pants
Bridal Knife
The Vig
Gore Horse
Heavy Horn
Plum Miser
Orb Lust
The Can Not
Jabber Jowl
Lurch Toward
Isolate Flecks
Down Chowder
Hate Park
All Hog
Change Banger
Clever Leper
Heorot Blonde
Gobs of Loss
Snarl Tart
Conference Motel
Solid Wiccan
The Plenty Dent
Ice Blunt
Hand Choke

The Deep Lawn
Lemmy Chin
Pound Sign
Gripe Style
Shy Right Hand
Cable Splicer
Level Mess
Skull Lesson
Code Ghost
The Coat Roll
Kept Exit
Man Ruse
Fact Sassy
Dying Flies
The Square Dunce
Dead Lumber
Alpha Bet
Celine Waste
Drudging Thru
Clobber Rob
Hawk Clot
Bad Vegan
Solo Cub
Yellow Bee
Penny Yen
Tent Trig
Dirge Version
Clark Can't
Charity Gall
Ether Cheat

The Rib System
Holy Loincloth
Vintage Chin
Same Candy
The TV Glow
Verb Perfect
Part Sickle
Trip Middle
Goat God
Smashed Uncle
Cross Lozenge
Tabby Cat
Seven Feathers
El Heady
OK Pressure
Radio Waiting
The Ocean Floor
Merman Hellville
Fur Stitches
Hoarding Lovely
Harp Poon
Lowbrow Hope
Knife Toe
Prison Mom
Whale Oil
Fail Boat
Damp Ham
Safe Caper
Saturn Cash
Clatsy Pine

Klepto Vet
Mince Mints
Spell Treasure
Red Bevel
Very Martian
Sea Mobsters
Proper Not
Hop Pot
Pollack Car
Third Sunspot
Pep Leopard
Clobber Dark
Total Knobs
Replay Kennedy
Choose Moose
Rue Tootsie
Chet Selection
Mime Arrival
Gate Player
New Lent
Beneath Bleachers
Dove Diversion
Zoo Dye
Nordic Mustache
Walrus Action
The Great Big Temptation
Milo Riot
The Best Same
Beggar Question
Divorce Chorus

Churns with Cream
Baby Saber
Mega Set
The Drunk Best Man
Kept Debt
#Stoners
Dread Better
Glide Timer
Lender Dirt
Truck Shovels
Cake David
Wing Free
Proper Cops
Relative Fade
Hint Nympho
Craig Leftover
Cubed Pluto
Crock Bot
Certain Birds
The Price of Kevin
Sham Plan
The Got Nozzle
Skin Dent
The Sniper Type
Glum Lumps
Spools of Juice
Jam Condor
Scan Tron
Sweet Beelzebub
Diaper Fire

Sin Cleanser
Guest Settler
Chant Standard
Whiff of Tinsel
Nag Wagon
The Bed Get Through
Shoo Vikings
Perfume Soup
Chill Missile
The Very Trap
Black Gag
Vegas Blessing
Surge Texture
Jeff Fresh
Tie Pride
The Budge Nevers
Coal Bluster
Tourniquet Swelling
Bailing Out Troy
Mugger Certain
Toll Bloke
The Guess Wedges
Summer Hump
Dine In
Verb Sherbet
The Meander Can
Champion Nose
Scar Lard
Conjure Llama
Gross Cleaver

Tap Patter
Bale of Failure
Roads to Pave
Neck Western
Char Garden
Us Wussy
Street Sleet
Fang Danger
Chamber Slur
Small in the Distance
Space Braid
Tailor to the Stars
Web Sweater
Moon Tunic
Nessnessness
Cry Infanticide
Will Critter
Vroom Goon
Some Tuesday Later
Traffic Pig
The Stellar Morning
Groove Tumor
Practically Fort Worth
Expatriate Babies
Pill Rig
Bulls with Crude Oil
The Verge of Darwin
Portions of Pie
The Friars of Thee
Gum Drunk

The Selling Bell
Feather Belts
Short Coddle
Yo Fro
Gland Tantrum
Sob Goblet
Itch Blizzard
Worth Both
Black Toga
Maid Bombers
The Grew Tender
The Death Chubs
Pitch Black Fork
The Jinx Bee
The Moral Men
Robust Dibs
Clipped Gentry
The Comfortable Hum
Most Minor
The Fib Crib
Tank Lace
Gabber
Local Oink
Pit Tip
Church Pants
Soda Straw
Dip Hiccup
Pubic Domain
Pot Pipe
Bib Indent

Small in the Distance

"I have this new world inside of me"
is the idea that sprung to mind and so
I leapt at it, deer-posed, as if over
a wire fence. If it ran very far
over a field of dried brownish stuff
it might grow small in the distance,
off into the horizon slit. If I saddle
some beast and ride further, some pale
happiness might be found in a faraway
forest. But, it's not meant to be. You
can tell by the robes on the shoulders.
Also, the dress as it folds off her neck
and arms is really beautiful (depending
on your sense of beauty) but it's not
an opening to another dimension.
Obviously, how new dimensions form
is a matter of some of dispute, but
something more obvious bothers me.
How can I be a better person and how
can this new world grow if the wind
never howls, angular at the trees?
"Careful," you want to say, but you don't
say careful. You don't say anything
because you're being careful.

Coming Home Again

I kept opening the door and saying, "I'm home,"
and the people who greeted me kept greeting me
and each time it was new, but it felt like the last time.
"I'm home," I said and the door behind me swung shut
exactly in the manner I imagine it, a very wooden door,
the cold air of winter, the sound of a coat, the airwaves
pushed like stretchy hula hoops. There are even the sounds
of breath and of whispers and ideas. As a child you
might stamp your boots in the hallway by the back door
and as an adult you find yourself doing roughly the
same motion, in a kitchen, a different snowy wind.
"It is time for bed," you hear yourself saying and it is
time for bed. When you crawl into bed it is another
night that you are crawling into bed. When you wake
the next morning, extending your limbs to their limit,
yawning, slowly fumbling with your eyelid, it is always
like the other mornings you've awoken to. The memories
you launch, folded in a paper airplane. It's as if you say,
"Good luck, little buddy," and just let it go and out it drifts
over the canyon, over the river, over some wall.

Moon Toner
Loom Central
Juggle Girl
The Best Corn
Tag Alot
Lawn Alarm
Dot Bottom
Back Savage
Beret Parade
Cheers for Villains
Demigod Fog
Babe Corner
Straw House
Foundation of Sand
Rubber Drawbridge
Motivation Loafers
5 O'clock Shadow Boxing
The Butler Did It
Dread Box
Moxie Grease
Texas Fatso
Para Sights
The Seatbelt Lawyers
Cha Cha Monument
Heavy Brow
League Bourbon
Slurp Puppy
The Host of Hosts
Male Pattern
Scare Wolf

Easy Arson
The Grade Basin
New Sleeve Vapor
Stay Maker
Beard of Bees
Apple Halves
Come Here Lucifer
The Glad Fabric
Cop Trash
Enemy Heads
Trill Lizards
Coming Home Again
The Rib Bone Phone
Thick Butter
Low Lard
Sip Cashmere
Brain Casings
Prominent Douchebag
Goof Chooser
Slag Pile
Drizzler
Wreck Head Room
The No One Cheers
Kick Big Top
A Matter of Water
Bond Pony
Regress West
Large Barge
One Point Game
The Stress Dad

Cave Deferment
Tar Parlor
Black Clad
Rabbit Tooth
Clues to Mysteries
Mule Tutor
Goop Poor
Rust Pool Q
Game Stranger
Sight Titan
Door Bird
The Up Shod
Perk Church
Automatic Gift
Grit Quickly
Chill Tilda
Soft Lob
Clove Bow
The Perm Chair
Wimpy Sons
Midlife Rooster
The Thank-You Foxes
Lovely Stony
Veil of Pliers
Dead Bugs
Spring Leon
Teal Switchblade
Sexy Bear
The Chime I'm
Get Mitchell

Cheek Turns
Pedal Boat
The Sugar Ache
Stuffy Loaf
Slot Comma
The Love Mullets
Care Cherries
Sin Core
The Kinds of Sauce
Dull Luggage
Nylon Fingers
Curb Burro
Neighborhood Text
Talent Vapid
Jail & Toenails
Pester Less
The Dang Pains
Women Named Ronnie
Animal Ark
The Stateless Left
Polly Anna Phantom
The Clump Assumption
The Body of Lice
Karma Target
The Sample Teds
Exam Dandy
Clod Option
Hello Cello
Catching Flies
Camper Mum

Cripple Section
The Famous Yous
Meat Chopper
Serious Getter
Trick Pip
Super Bloom
Sick Jumper
The Respectable Hurt
Burly Curb
Scads of Rad
Neck Message
Blind Potter
Jets to Jerusalem
The War on Error
Table Sake
Whale Claw
Draw Rodger
Tart Practice
Keep Eve
Please Season
Christ Pilot
The Toledo Ants
Small Ear
Bundle Gun
Seven Kevins
Fringe Pixies
Flay Satans
Chance Cannibal
Ailing Rancher
The Lisping

Kissinger Accent
Legume Research
The Status Lattice
Rust Because
Ivy Rich
Steal Crystal
Box Job
Toll Malone
Mostly Kinda
Rag and Bone Man
Night Soil
Gift Snake
Classic Bad Guy
White Leather Vest
Clearly Murder
Jump High School
The Top Mom
Sup Brunette
The Eyebrow History
Dark Otter
Truck Pidgins
The Cheap Keep
Tweed Police
Creeper Speed
The Sample Pamphlets
The Knee Faces
Somewhat Family
The Fun Sums
Lake Age
Sin Planes

Hard Lot's Wife
Billions of Fireflies
Time Mites
Grind Alum
Large Wanda
Nietzche Peace Treaty
Grown-Up Problem
Stutterer
Otto Otto
Bluff Lover
All Stood Up
Topflight Buzz Saw
Back Strap
Two Million
The Eye Whites
Jewel Galoot
Thin Upper Lip
Button-Up Dress
Clone Arm
Darting Through Smog
Artifact Orphanage
Prelim Gin
The Reefer Beat
The Local Fuzz
Bequeath Tea
Brain Camper
So So Yoyo
Pal Salon
Finger Nip
Little Vicious Dogs

The Jealous Lot
Whisk Management
Bearskin Landing
Arch Seminal
Dork Court
The Sampson Pun
Sin Pinch
The Bit Stifle
Ad Lib Chisel
Grand Vandal
Vulgar Urge
Tremble Gimmick
Pundit Tummy
Near Pillage
Gun Mouth
Glass Starter
Bored Strumpet
Fig Mustang
Trigger Sick
Numb Sir
Wolf Bunker
Middle Brother
Bloody Ring Finger
Charm Barber
Tin Vow
Satan Drapes
Mall Cartel
Rubber Drugs
The Shove Bubbas
Aft Cap

Finch Dagger	Sank Bank
Seven Legs	Some Outfit
Pop Pill	A Bit Glib
Super Funeral	Spite Tiger
Banks Full of Locusts	Gulls Like Rosebuds
Scare Parable	Fun Enough
Flutes Made of Bourbon	The Astronaut Toss
Mother Soap	Golly Ball
Grey Mentor	Twin Swindle
New Gurney	Cardigan Wet Dream
Collar Hurt	Virgin Gumption
Dab Catcall	The Light Inside the Body
Feast Beast	Born Sorta
The Gleeson Knees	Perfect Germs
The End Times Kite	Slot Hockey
Blood Bowl	Drained Fat
Men Against Ham	The Bitty Boom
Brillo Cad	Cobra Butt
Chop Happy	Cumber Bunny
The Scab Cab	Black Cattle
Frilly Shirtsleeves	Power Foot
The Tea Gives	Bailiff Cowlick
Crowded Placard	Ch-Ch-Choose Me
Nuke Salute	The Bounce Pass
Paper Favor	Devin Headjob
Ant Clarity	Barn Fro
Candid Didn't	Tackle Cab
The Ill Market	Groom Nerves
Dreg Melon	Tan Gent
Diversion Birth	Slat Past

Greet Sleet
Pea Size
Page Rehearsal
One Onion
Overt Said So
Fab Bath
Cast Limbs
Alt Salt
Coma Splice
Litter Bit
Chem Burn
Zent
Quick Kick
Cash Taffy
Ow Bow
Hornet Sweater
Guest Cop
Coping Thug
Jut Gut
Tile Bison
Slow Dough
They Worry
Extravagant Brag
Juice Fart
Torso Corp
All Dealio
Churn Vermin
Swear Lords
Teen Smirks
Burst Stunt

Studied Ed
Pose Loaded
Vivid Cheat
Curly Head
Coal Toe
Grizzly Ump
Back Vein
Pig Bladder
Pox House
Option Cask
Text Jet
Flag Fire
Upper Chomps
The Did Sea
Phillip Gas
Mars Swarm
Lindy First Kiss
Pent Down
Long Brown
Mid Cookie
Supreme Pug
The Jump Somewhat
Given Pit
Dumb Friends
European Socialism
Muzzle Cup
Nail Gun Animal
Feature Piece
Gender Quilt
Kilo of Oil

Quincer
Sponge Darts
Pat Relaxer
Rafter Calf
Clamp Band
Mist Tizzy
Pon Tiff
Roll Ghosts
Thunder Sunk
Drab Slab
Slap Henry
Lad Paddle
Gummy Hum
Terse Earl
Wide Suit Jacket
Navy Slate
The Turn Toward
Grand Swank
Hawk Bargain
The Lesser Lease
The Nothing Goes
Told Baloney
Nub Crud
Leopard Arp
Splat Gnat
Leopold Wasteland
You Proof
Snow Flare
Cardinal Win
Deep Blank Garage

The Stress Economy
Brave Ever After
Brown-Eyed Handsome
  Gems
One-Hand Shotgun
Hooker's Dead Partner
Gambler Hamper
The Can't Money
The Man Who Killed Johnny
Grasping at Gauze
Cameo Fan
A Terrific Marriage
Herer
Bog Caveat
Beer Cleats
Gin Scoop
Hoof Bruise
Hipper Wiggle
Straight Craze
Eye Black
Hog Tog
Gutter Frog
Lightly Toast
Heavy Mouser
Nadine Mean
Powder Foundation
Hull Solid
How Marvelous
Heel Chop
Thunky

Dual Roxie
99 Cents
The Same Canary
One Car Dark
Some Nolan
Gush Socket
Almond Butter
Room Moor
Tiger Baskets
Gift Shank
New Rude
Nude Rue
Killed Looter
Truth Trough
Suffixerer
7 Different Zones
Late CDs
The Lament Edge
Hurt Leg
Barren Wedding Bed
Dob of Partly
Big Round Circles
Arto Dresso
Jarm
New Troy
More Compact
Close Bosom
Modernity Whiz
Collapse Parka
Journey Furnace

Oodles Looser
Big Spork Field
Playing Dr. Phil
Muse Critics
Smaple
Machine Wind
Bad Singer
Spark Shower
Doll Lopped Off
The Cast of Grease
Mangler Bird
The Full Looting
Hang Loveray
Super Bathing Suit
Mouse Organ
Leather Italy
Pressed Legroom
What's Best for Me
Good Fabric Bad
Instep Whip
Benny Hands
Chester Because
Pull Elastic
Gab by Steeple
Beams of Teamwork
All Jailer
Foot Scripture
Ample Gram
Swing Work
Full Pander

More Compact

There was a man who drove a moped
and worked as a bee for a living.
He would buzz around and feel achy and loose.
He annoyed anyone listening, anyone paying
attention. At night he'd come home
and say to his wife, "Lord! Working
like this is going to kill me." And she'd say,
"Is it really?" And he'd say, "It sure is."
And she'd say, "Or is it?" And he'd say, "Sure,
sure it is." And she'd say, "Or is it?"
And he'd say, "O, it is." In the morning he'd
fasten his lacquered helmet and watch
for traffic. At work, he tried to be better,
buzzing harder, flying faster, being a tinier
bee than before, more compact.
But nothing good came of it.
It was a long time later, when he'd retired,
that his wife said, "Lord! You being home
like this is going to kill me." And he said,
"It sure is," and shut the door quietly.

Foreign Object

It was nowhere to be found. Neither
was the woman. She was nowhere. She
was nowhere and we couldn't find
her. Or it. We were looking earnestly.
I even took it seriously. But there was
nowhere to take it from there. From
there, there was just nothing. So
after a point, we gave up. One person
looked at me and I looked back
and we said, "That's it." So, there it was,
nowhere. I had something in my shoe
and slipped it off like I was removing
a gun from a gun case. Deep inside
the dark area where sunlight couldn't
fall, I could sense a foreign object, not
as big as a thumb, but no smaller than
a pupil. "What pupil?" said a voice from
within. Without realizing it, I was
answering, "The one you're not using."
That was all clear enough. "It's true," said
another voice. This voice put my shoe
back on. The next voice I heard was
your voice and it said, "What voice?"

Smarten Upstairs
Friends Cheering
The Comp End
Foreign Object
Zimmerman Pancakes
The Check Beg
The Assistant Golf Pro
Cloud White Suit
Rang Finger
The Upper Down
Itchy Dawn
Trophy Life
Bright Stars Named Clio
Mink Keeper
Not About the Future
Purpose Sore
The Heart-Shaped Pool
Water Nighter
Point Ander
Stall Mallard
Nile Plywood
El Jamboree
Stand Offish
Cab Elbow
The Milling Room
Daddy Pacing
Cool Nook
Chile Will
The Blanket Dangle
Tar Plode

Goose Digit
Lank Pentecost
Dud Mallet
Do Rose
Clack Hat
The Grocery Cartel
Hinder Nun
Yearn Bikini
Root Beer
Chant Camp
Loose Noose
Rope Hardener
Shit Possum
Circular Fern
Fan Belter
Jehovah Deep Throat
Ham Turnstile
Fruit Equipment
Blender Perverts
Bong Tongs
Red Fur Coat
Gloat Rover
Nope Halo
June Two Belts
Nevada Ass
Glide Bible
Waste War
Pendenter
Share Careful
Tongue Almond

Ditch Victor
Smart Lard
Prim Gimp
Holy Polly
The Murphy Church Pew
Grant Mantis
Fat Cheeks
Blazing ATV
The Riddle Grill
Candid Shave
Trace Ringlets
Barter Yarn
Teaming D
Talcum Setback
Gopher Soul
Dirt Young
Cold Mention
Janitor Sampson
Glam Detour
The Mutt Shut Up
Quinn Skin
Destination Placemat
Sap Papa
Milo Dander
Utility William
Paper Platter
Hut Hut Hike
Snail Tailor
Yes Dominant
Feckless Kettle

Crème de le Crimp
Feather Chester
Cough Wheat
Head Staples
Petro Necklace
Rudder Gorgeous
AKA Crypt
The Shape of a Cape
Derby Logic
The Handle Dizzy
Lunk Funky
Greet Fink
Able Bent
Bleach Drinker
Factor Blackball
Yellow Rainstorm
Middle Gearbox
Tamara Gamble
Number Abe
Life Force Boredom
The Groan Float
Edgy Pets
Hard Black
Rile Bye-Bye
Fugitive Pidgin
Gape Western
Fine Diner
Prism Lent
Capone Undershirt
Act Timeout

Signs of Acupuncture
Cave Spacing
Brick Pill
Shy Gadget
The Opt Out
Glitter Rigor
The Cid Herd
Blemish Inch
Long Green Walls
Boulder Vie
Simple Peaches
Sin Quiver
Swim Whither
Lather Saddle
Fib Kicker
The Can Stance
Famine Lamb
Charging Roulette
Sexy Bike Ride
The Went Button
Sham Murder
Con Target
Viola Stint
Wiper Outer
Cyanide Bombshell
Cardboard Owl
Coffee Larva
Shut Vulcan
Arson Padre
Packing Saul

Jefferson Harpooner
Chat Pigtails
Grog Sock
Chalk Strumpet
Hang Panel
Relief Hicks
Taker Ape
Boat Toad
Ill Teddy
Forger Rodent
Roy Returns
Preppy Guest
Super Beautiful
Local Costume
Fang Sander
Sans Haggard
Banned Textbooks
Sham Diaphragm
Third Period Math
Hi Einstein
Spear Teardrop
The Never Johnny Cougar
The Probate Sort
The Perfectly Hurt
Sailing Toward Hail
Jar Carp
Wax Meal
Kevlar Bowtie
Bone Cupcake
The Better Best

Slid Twenty
Garble Hard
Pages of Destiny
Shag Slipup
Rug Deal
Prison Fist
Shady Guru
Gift Shop Copper
Leeway Sweetheart
Ape Tooth
Invisible Empty
The Leak Keyhole
Wonder Foot
Phase Liver
The Dilate Alice
Comfort Jeans
Chapter Book
Sexy Shirt
Nerd Telescope
Tad Vacant
Hitchcock Tits
Blunt Tutor
Foxy Catacomb
The Science Hips
Crib Madison
From Greta
The Zoo Truthers
Dark Slop
Bar Rage
The Sift Gritty

The Delete Tease
Early Mummy
Neighbor Liaison
Wet Robe
Rope Hand
Quitter Legroom
The Happier Mask
Lest Faceless
Room Toodle
Sheer Licorice
Pantsuit Device
Liable Tyrant
Mideast Whistle
The Darling Stomp
Wire Choir
The Mission Amp
A Larger Register
Teller Meltdown
Romeo Broom
The Deny Supply
Meek Simmer
Told Float
The Soup News
Chance of Thunder
Part Slobber
Soot Loophole
Bloody Kettle
Vigor Figure
Direct Meerkat
The Choke Vocation

Neck Twister
Blood Florida
Freeze Keeper
Valid Jab
The Crayfish Issue
The Plus Tortoise
Yank Eloise
The Jamie Cellar
Torn Landry
The Lay-Down Caper
The So-So Mope
Dimmer Temple
Rabbi Goodvibe
Soul Holder
Ban on Everything
Getting Last
Couch Goodbyes
Baby Hearts
Pill Cups
Slant Antler
Mona Ghost
A Change in Vampires
Hawkeye Plight
Echo Aren't
Screen Wrinkle
Riser Silence
Squid Guilt
Rum Apron
Argyle Shortstop
Scarf Larva

Mirror Lira
Polio Child
Antenna Kin
The Moon Perk
Gig Sis
Cheap J
Chance Anagram
Carver Callous
Slant Mandate
The Thankless Tamper
Creek Igor
The Jump Plummet
Gaffe Fab
Stagger Gust
The Him Limpers
Cord Mort
Clay Deathtrap
The Could Always Sue
Chamber Weed
The Glove Cupboard
Your 2nd PhD
Gizz Juzzler
Up Tupper
Interloper Sir
Very Rare Scare
Handlebar Montage
Loretta's Dresses
Igh Eels
Landlord Android
Gatlin Pun

Shank Hard
Norb Dust
Forked Merlin
Sprawl Dogs
Mirror Queer
Double Fidgets
The Blah Factor
Brag Cartel
Dirty Garçon
Jitter Crib
Should Chipper
Kilos of Gravy
Zero Summer
Bard Hardhat
Gargler
Ring Around the Dollar
Potato Purpose
Birdie Murder
Howboy Cat
Arrow Fire
The Mission Remainder
Chest Hair Mess Up
Ditto Hit
Germ Sponge
Hitler Pistol
The Mingus Tingle
Rope Belt
The Ref Nothing
The Tow Whole
Jaw Baseball

The I've Connive
Tried Lightly
The Offer Loft
Gave Basement
Chat Bat
Nice Tassels
Mile Pliers
Handy Damsel
Channel Grind
Tinkers with Mars
Ice Viola
Rush Boot
Keel Heel
Garner Star
The Bro Pastor
Fade Taser
Love Brah
Trauma Rasta
Dobby Mob
Mate Rotator
Club Incidentally
Seep Finger
Gwen Hiccup
Myriad Reaper
Public Connection
The Give Super
The Well Melt
Augustine Debtor
Plywood Knives
Rink Feather

Black Satin Jackets
Grease Eagles
Barber Jobs
Door Sturgeon
The Bigger Clique
Cinch Grin
Nail Jailer
Tad Rash
Born Cheetah
Tummy Full of Thumbs
A New Winga
Mother Gambler
Visions of Geese
Stream Meat
Cadaver Lass
Heavyweight Universe
Eleven Eons
Char Between
Freezer of Limbs
Grass Flagger
Bipedal Ledger
Grist History
More Del Shannon
Tall Milk
The Shill Prep
Cling Blinker
Taste Vagrant
Bunk Gumbo
The Boo Cue
Screw Tulip

Sand Jersey
Summer Claw
Bus Women
Ink Lease
The Would-Be Mob
The Cannot Lamb
Nin Sin
Yester Beer
The Shame Ham
Flea Meister
Chill Gizmo
Tank Headache
Slang Mustache
Puss Mugger
Grammar Dram
Dank V
Vader Helmet
Clue User
Deep Bedpan
Ship Python
Omni Omen
Ploy Yoko
Twig Signet
Massive Raft
Roller Bloke
Stick Kiss
Biscuit Bag
Lead Beak
Ruffle Breast
Rifle Tyke

The Detective People
Robuster
Mud Pummel
Locust Goat
Meager Sweets
The Possible Ops
Tang Milkshake
The 1970s TV Cops
Posh Hot
Shush Hoodlum
Roof Gondola
Your Friend's Big Sister
Pinker Envy
A Fourth Man
Data Backdrop
The Silly Blahs
Lob Cottage
Fly Wide
Softball Girls
Maine Vacation
Gore Endorser
The Universal Coronet Game
The Historic Torque
Slam Manner
Chunk Moto
Mirror Gibbon
Trucker Jokes
Hefty Meth
Not Bloody Yet

Yolk Ball
Mega Feta
Tokyo Cola
Iron Hairnet
Bellicose Coda
Pious Convention
Ernest Mole
The Tomorrow Owl
Cafeteria Fire
King Childless
My Kinky Dank
Moral Lapdog
Agnes Vista
Checker Pellet
Mullet Sedan
The Highly Groomed
Learning to Mow
Coat Hung
Race Cradle
Juke Tutor
Stopper Salt
Drab Quagmire
Harried Candidate
Unglued Falcons
Clutter Mutt
The Might Vilify
Pump Wire
Coy Yodel
Bogart Tart
Attack Flasher

A Fourth Man

"I'm not the father I'd like to be," said
the man who was taller than the man
he was speaking with. "Oh?" said the
shorter man. "Yes," said the taller man.
"I'd like to be a father who is taller."
"Oh?" said the shorter man, "You're
all ready quite tall." "Oh, yes, I know,"
said the taller man. "But still, something
inside of me longs for something in that
next layer of air, that next foot or so
above me." "It's an odd problem," says
a third man, somewhat fatter than both
men. "Oh?" says the tallest man. "Well,
rather, it's an odd yearning. It's like
a cat who falls in love with a balloon."
"Truly, sir," said the short man, "You are
indeed speaking my language now."
"Oh?" said the tall man, "Do you mean like
how a button, say, in your overcoat
might, say, I don't know, want to conquer
things and attacks the bread toaster first,
as if the bread toaster were all evil and
the coat button were all good? Or do
you mean like how a short, tall and
fat man might want to confer and yet

they find there is no big umbrella for
them all to fit under?" "It is a tragic event,"
said a fourth man. This man was dressed
in wool and looked a little like an armadillo.
"It is my understanding," he began, but
the others were turning toward the sun now.

The Defeat Meter
Left Odder
Troll Lawyer
Muddy Subtle
Proud Ouster
Loco Florist
Dither Weirdly
Hence Mickey
Ten Feet Higher
Critical Foot Rub
Deputy Snub
West Shredder
Bing Feast
Bad Otter
Traipsing Through Utilities
Judge Pudgy
O Raul
Trek Sector
Thor Dumpling
The Gel Letters
Early Man Ray
Dice Tiny
Suspender Men
The Kalamazoo Work Cycle
Flapper Past
The Costello Rosins
Thin Gold Necklace
Rabbit Eyes
The Decreasement
Family Rancher

Diss Kitchen
Tour Goshen
Calf Lies
Barrymore Roulette
The Given Nixons
Roosevelt Totals
Pal Balance
Burlapper
Hot Shop
Wolf Dick
Bat Ratchet
The Long Kid Time
Sax Candle
The Sheen Trident
Custom Dustup
Jean Jacket Bad Guy
The Sink Goes
Roll Lotus
Champ Mario
Grog Toggle
The Zombie Throb
Ain't Milk
Fat Fleet
Blear Weakness
Sleek Me Too
The Blue Right Now
Luxury Ono
Nose Meat
Minus Lifetime
Regular Updo

Cinch Fidel	Gums Under
Wet Rug	Starry Back
The Steer Clearer	Quilt Liver
Chemo Meow	Knee Jesus
Stagger Prone	Till Anger
Too Tutu	Searching for Robots
Barcode Pony	Pipe Fight
Considering Gym Class	Juniper Piston
The Buy Tiger	Cast Bun
Thief Wrist	Pearl Slingshot
Car Chase Scenes	Almost Doing It
The Classic Blackout	The Done Its
Stunt Busing	Out of Place Shrubs
Flat Box	Bald Cartoon
Cigar Rags	Gas Private
The Plummeting Price	Vetted Clever
Dash Pillowcase	The Will of the Bank Tube
Metal Cassettes	A Place of Business
Viper Buyer	Status Quo Moat
Nail Gunner	Trevor Whatever
Mummy Big Time	Slog Pogrom
Ready Ever After	The Worse Toaster
Dent Dripper	Blink Fit
Pretending to Live	TV Parents
Gab Casket	Quantity Programing
Project Fop	Sever Gelding
Fully Clad Cad	Surf Rudolph
Rochester Mice	The Back Ninety
Double Ginger	Wag Sandstorm
Chavez Operative	The Lots of Dots

Caddy Badger
Sheetrock Sadness
Goat X-Ray
Bread Flesh
Orange Blobs
The Rest Zoom
Bade Open
Pie Kiosk
The New Car Melt
Rose Mooing
Gawk Hawks
Shapes the Roadmap
Snot Cow
The Moo Goose
The Drum Sums
The Retie Mighty
Scarves Like Wildfire
Scratch Fast
The Me Weakness
French Fences
Kip Meter
The Jar Nasty
Lump Pogo
Larger Hindu
Hardest Cabbage
The Invest Lecture
Page Ricochet
Rad Comment
Cob Sapper
The Loin Joint

Cloth Beak
The Relief Echoes
Fretless Bed
The Smooth Truly
Permanent Nit
Grief Feeder
Plume Union
Cooler Suit
Sad Flagship
Batter Snatcher
Evade Caver
Bruise Eater
Log Raccoon
Messed-Up Delegate
Pamper Clamp
Master David
Deacon Butcher
Tell Madame
The Promptly Gave
Favor Prince
Maid Secret
Midas Eardrop
The Isn't Willed
A Strong Normandy
Born Gascon
The Agony Trying
The Faint Tincture
A Flickering Light
Dare Parish
The Hawk Character

The Cleric Swear
Glutton Killer
The Mingle Weep
Proof Reaper
Busy Fellows
Divided by Z
Meeker Actress
The Bury Carriage
Such Shaky Ground
The Rattle Reeds
Elephant Shop
Pairs with Doubt
Mist Buzz
Cease Too Soon
Extract Magma
The Fidelity Force
Parliament Holiday
Latter August
Lord North's Despair
Idle Teaching
The Been-There Lloyd's
The Review Etc.
Perfect Boats
Heard Ravens
Leech Teacher
The Alas Gentleman
Plumb Hens
In Small Green
Till Dinner
Shrub Bluff

Doom Blossom
The Broom Resort
Further Corpses
Blight Outright
Miserable Sleep
Gold Veins
Parted Robert
Trick Jugular
The Bells Declare
Renewal Sky
Whistle History
The Meager Village
Lamp Out
The Against Moneys
Unusual Aces
Duel Pushkin
47,000
The Many Pious
The Seized Me
Glory Horn
The Own Nothing
The Evidence Against Us
The Scuffle Toward
Constable Horatio
Book Gazettes
Rope Coil
Starry Garb
Prefix Vehicle
Pedantic Streak
Irritating Juxtaposition

Nay Occasional
Certain Negatives
A Plato Transplant
Evoked by Something
Lady's Fan
Enigma Account
The Normal Coexist
Muddy Purple
Dumb Gestures
The Hurry Home Boy
The Contrary Lengthwise
Forehead Horror
The Meanwhile Accuser
A Gasp or Two
Milk Thug
The Bid Promptly
Bull Youth
Thick Wet Dream
Quality Thief
Thigh Meat
The Tricky Skinny
The Puff Shoulder
The Once Dry Hair
Shitty Fingernails
Oil Peel
The Strange Generous
The Three Worst Lucifers
Judas Brutus
Strange BMXers
The Shrink Back

O Light Supreme
Swine Deaf
The Loyal Ado
The Gracious Chase
Token Noble
The Or Stubborn
Kiss Plenty
The Fifi Willing
Rude Witch
The Befall Chapel
Lace Knot
False Faith
O Stuntman
Karate Forecast
The Prove Obstinate
Kook Wolf
The Fond Fight
Pet Forest
With Whom We Slept
Husband Glare
Less Reasonable Creatures
The Spouse How-To
Chide Violence
The Luck Pretext
Chrome Hearse
Acid Tongue
The Almighty Reckon
The Give-In Bit
Pert Feather
Gut Mill

The Pope Himself
The Other Killed
Sorrow Pump
Socrates Wives
Unhappy Scholar
A Chance for Rioting
Police Victims
Sheesh Minefield
Babe Wait
Motorbike Pyro
The Just Wants
Pleaser Shin
Cross Hospital
Yield Keeper
Curt Pop Star
The Very Very Close
Wood Water
Puzzles of Winter
The Bus Interaction
Finals LeBron
Chat Alfred
Zealot Bell
Fight Tin
Cabinet Lies
Beak Stoppage
Equally Cruel
The Ever Silent Strove
Dim Sea
Subdue Port
The Lulu Vessels

Battle White
Noble Furrows
O Priestess
Death Vault
A Worthy Glow
Phantom Bear
The Sorrow Yew
The Babbling Flash
Rubbish Eggs
The Pile Complete
What God Have Made
Nature Pang
The Futile Sooth
The Gather Alter
Clog Merry
The Wordy Vigor
Feud Speech
Party Strife
Love's Dumb Cry
The Faithless Cold
Civic Slander
Spite Ring
The Keen Seize
Dug Central
Shock Fawn
Christ Mold
The Blind Clamor
Noble Ends
Hissing Tears
Cyclic Bike

The Freezing Reasons
Epilogue Fog
Foam Grape
Ample Tracts
The Ever-Breaking Shore
Droopy Moms
The Scope Ought
Hoary Burr
Crutch Yuck
Shame Ban
Skull Laugh
Dwindle Imps
The Sorta Catch
Stiff Blind Horse
Hoof Fiend
Toe Brute
Struggle Dunce
A Life Spent Training
Mad Brewage
Footstep Further
Mock Squat
Abolitionist Kid
Drederick Fouglass
The Prophet Wants
The Correct Opinion
Gone Long Before
The Seldom Cherry
Cushy Permission
The Natural Affection
Hinder Champ

More Hammer All Lee
Duration Page
Wicked Bigger
Implicit Lick
The Great House Lloyd
Jargon Badge
The Often Few
Scarce Flesh
Yankee Adjunct
The Cannot Shaken
Broadcloth Star
The Peg Creed
Ice Cheat
Sick Elk
Dress War
Between Boots
The Own Notion
The Original Discord
Meager Sting
Erect Keg
The Nor Gingham
The Fitful Events
Burly Chap
The Second Dogwatch
Rumor Overcoat
Official Pyramid
Fever Crook
The Snuff Drunk
Order Fox
Bug Supper

The Way to Drowsy
Stretch Eleven
Sermon Ornament
The Collar of Lice
Modern Doubt
A Pissed Luther
Ball Face
Plague Fleas
The Equally Well
The Blade End
Thousand Dollar Revenge
Dud Cub
Skirmish Skirt
The Undysfunction
The Behind Mileage
The Former Former
The Agony Combat
Thirst Sitter
King Stingy
The Get Loot
Toenail Paint
Black Midriff
The Impale Horn
Rob Lots
Contempt Grin
The Melissa Childhood
Caesar Knees
Claw Adder
O Beautiful Cruel
Lover Backhoe

Stud Relaxer
Fathers and Daughters
Thy Cap
Household Spies
Raw Moth
Chariot Heart
The Lower Coy
Skull Squisher
Fatted Calf
A Heap of Nonsense
Lightshow Backdrop
Over Sixteen
Blackbird Pie
A Sudden Pox
Great Philosophers
The Prophet Beards
The Church Rump Roast
The Single Lofty
The Bishop of Paris
Wine Liberties
The Pear Lecture
Select Pest
Enormo Codpiece
Between Frances
Coffee Rook
The Mint Purse
Dagger War
Guide Rope Stuff
French Inch
Fruit Permit

Fathers and Daughters

There was a girl named Rose who felt
a sadness in her wrist bones that hurt her
deeply. She said to her father, "Dad, can
we visit a surgeon, or something? This
sadness in my wrist bones is hurting me
deeply." Her father didn't have lungs
and so all of his breath had to swim
through gills. He gave her a look that
said, "Listen, though we all have sadness
lodged somewhere inside us, the sadness
of gills is the real sadness. The sadness
in your wrist bones will disappear once
you have followed the instructions,
felt the volume of your eyes, weighed
and measured the pockets of resistance
in your palms." She considered this carefully,
imagining the way sadness might attach
itself to a little buggy and be trotted away
with an echoing sound. "But my wrist bones,"
she said. His gills were quivering. The air
between them like a silent giant.

The Prettiest Bloom

Leroy was with me and
he said, "Check the blossom
on that blossom."
He was referring to
this particular rose
in a particular bunch
of roses. Leroy had good
ideas about the world
so I looked and protruding
out of that particular
rose was a finger and
it was pointed at me.
I said, "Whoa, Leroy!"
But he was already
saying, "I know."
Both of us were just
paralyzed, standing
accused.

Root Grab
Taut Crossbows
The Wet Eighty
Filthy Views
Legal Fees
Thicker Strike
The Stay Away Dogs
Sour Bombs
They Pray
Even in the Grave
The Better Demise
Cousin Vulture
Title Woe
The Late Fling
Gate Slave
Quixote Whirl
Himself God
The Dead Man Would
Pro Monk
The Prettiest Bloom
Hazard Order
Wit Mister
Whereupon the Hunger
A Debt Blessing
The Invoke Wait
Money Gunn
Fact After
The Entire Inquire
To Barely Ease
The Anonymous Kit

Wig Dyes
The Cute Amuse
Esteem Fink
Latter Zappa
Stone Dig
The Proper Gospel
A Fond Beer
These Reptiles
Joke Gearshift
The Keeps Cheating
The Rank Itself
Late Venue Snag
Twark Main
The Sir Excuse Me Sir
The Persecute Pitch
Gang Abyss
Vice Vibe
Defraud Rocco
Luggage Suede
Hook Goo
Trouble Melodrama
Street Litter
The Prize Plague
The Next Orion
Cake Sailor
Clipper Pit
Prince of Suitors
Murmur No
The Wraith Cars
Finished Issue

The Ice-Cream Stand
    Closes
Teenage Leo
Ivy Part
Creak Easter
The Hope Bestow
A Quaid Cop
All Python Aquarium
Montage Lessons
Kissing in Swimsuits
Behind Certain Phrases
The Movie Punk Rockers
Perfect Blue Mohawk
The Personalized High
    Fives
Hubcap Head Platter
Shirtless Buddy
Tank Candy
Ex Fest
Jesse Mandible
Fry Cook
Ask As Is
Drive Thru Order
Extra Thresher
Baby Helmets
Premier Needs
The Husky Because
Bro School
The Teens Weeping
Whirring Sounds

Slush Pile
Man Isle
A Carefully Planned
    Kidnapping
Cordless Homeroom
Gab Baptist
Strong Outer Wall
The Minute Siege
Good Ski Mask
Her Blue Heels
Safety Pillowcase
Snack Past
Pssst Listen
Known Wow
Scope Open
Sneer Lip
Fur Face
Half Flag
King Finger
Headless Noble
Fritter Awe
Neck Request
Beggar Lets
Ivory or Ivy
Maker Odd
The Fake 1,000
Stoned to Death
Round Face
Oil Bowl
The Avow Ouch

Cliff Wing
Bygone Fly
Drunken Huggers
Sweet Mess
The Dribble Kill
Rascal Salt
Gold Robes
Domino Goal
New Breed Apex
Swear Weather
Candlelit Bar
Jag Gadget
Unsold Dagger
Gus Slender
The Wide Enemy Shoes
Jank Spice Rack
Snow Cupcakes
The Substantial Yawn
Supergroup LP
Foil Cheek
Cape Fortnight
Nano Sanity
The Axe Violent
The Grey Subtext
Iron Tee Shirt
Glee Gore
The Don't Try
Police Bunny
The Very Concerto
Marine Mouse

The Giant Stadiums
Wimp Picnic
Striped Orange Spine
Neighbor Girl
Sharp Sleeves
Album Art
Po Biz
The Anti-Dahmer Faction
Pairings Included
Light Fixture
Eye Drop
Anchor Smell
The Blow Hardly
Throne Season
Jude the Obtuse
Civic Given
Glide Politely
Rowboat Wedge
Aqua Primates
Bad Posture
High School Sandals
Rosin Paddle
Keyboards in the Early 80s
Brake Dancer
Rubble Mustard
Cornice Gluten
The Barely Share
Tongue Stripe
Neck Licker
Labor Roast

Sister Tennis
A Sylvia Criminal
Sea Roll
Kept Bed
The Royal Sleep In
Pattern Fat
Blabber Lips
The Zip Shut
Ugh Christopher
Head Freckle
Natural Pistol
Western Bugger
Stick Thicket
Your Own Damn Car
Oil Pedal
Jealous Leg
Coral Totals
Spoon Prank
Snuck Gum
Easy Texas
Knuckle Braids
Crush Mutt
Num Chuck Likey
Powder Marlow
Bet Relic
Bee Growth
Ruse Crusade
Stab Bats
Permit Term
Cedric Request

To Hell Safely
Middle Kid Talent
Nurse Thief
Bowl Carver
Our Sour
Doll Crowd
Cave Mouser
Drugstore Odes
Dummy Press
Surplus Blur
Wood Eye
Dire Preacher
Burr Kilroy
Plastic as Gas
Hotel Fort
Moon Goof
Winter Gills
Blubber Coat
Dozer Hopeful
Gamer Champ
Paper Kate
Envy Tin
Soda Bottle
Sin Ear
Mute Bug
Change Drawer
Clean Salt
Tuesday Drug
Pig Sip
Local Shovel

Gravel Bedtime
Crank Dud
Broken Others
Stories About Quicksand
The Directors of
 Photography
World Record Holders
Ceiling Stars
Murder Research
Collar Buttons
Hurt Reasons
Dollar Higgins
Flare Gun Summer
The Pie Right Now
Comrade Origami
Nervous Above Us
Sorry Adam
Horse Disease
Wire Flag
Women in Trains
How Commie
Brass Rake
Full Length Nobody
Babe Fiancé
Sank Frinatra
Rubber Flow
Combat Wine
Javelin Teddy Bear
Lovable Mother
Jefferson Tart

Under Tim
The Principle Squeamish
Biter Mouth
Spilt Tooth
Root Cat
Pear Chin
Rain Do
King Stepchild
Ball Galoshes
Petty Letdown
The Give Shoulder
A Sexy Couple Years
Shaky Good Shaky Bad
Period Do
Illu Minate
Goodtime Rockslide
Nepal Gumbo
Clapper Nap
Honing Thorns
Groom Loop
Swoop Pool
New Canner
Pan Luster
Stumbles a Bit
Date Palladium
Chemical Tail
Dirt Mart
Proto Blunder
Pleather Face
Purge Banjo

Game Rubber
Dendrite Fire
Maritime Win
The Within Grid
Amino Minnow
The Stop Falling
Harried Church
Broke Turnip
Blood from a Stone
Proud Diver
Perfect Legroom
Hit Redo
Plush Druggie
The Pull Witness
Backseat Good
Hose Plosion
Gross Corset
Trim Shot
Tender Seeya
Vision Plumber
Saying Goodbye to the
    Internet
School Fussing
Inside Fly
Bad Physics
Dumb Turnout
Open Loser
Coast Grover
Harlem Sneakers
Mammoth Hunt

President Won't
Turn Feline
Earth Tub
P for Now
Plus Minus
One Pair of Broncos
Churchill Zubba
Screenplay Debacle
Lost Fathers
The Current Cutoff
Knifemare
Really Akimbo
Cotton Knees
Raccoon U-Boat
Genghis Below
Gum Swap Handshake
Third Moto
Pre-Microwave
Vary Hard Toenails
Venice Footfall
Putin Bitch
Clincher Kiss
Extra Loudest
The Anything Weapon
Shoots Midair
Given Chamberlain
Bipolar Jokes
Cheap Cashews
The Buzz Classic
Glenda Wish

Wooden Q
Tomorrowly
The Away Desk
Depression Lesson
Blink Maid
Rum Monk
Water Mars
Omen Note
Burly Truck
Supper Guppies
Snow Leotard
Cutthroat Jehovah
Nine Month Message
Wiccan Dentist
An Appropriate Roof
Kentucky Luck
Core Orca
Tremendous G
Urn Legs
Handsome Penmen
The Perfect Religion
Charisma Guild
Umbrellas Like Spiders
Gloat Robot
Gobber
Actuary Violence
Like There's No Tomorrow
Dullard Champs
The Image of a Train
The Underwater Scene

Brave Dickens
Two Ton Antler
Missing Wink
Expensive New Glasses
Fox Cone
The Refuse Service
Neck Attachments
Crouton Tusk
Yum Work
Really Deb
Dead Friends
Sniff Brisket
Rim Shark
Stuffed Grail
Moran Lawn
DMV Pal
Shifty Trustees
Jung Rug
Stereo Relish
Thimble Full of Fur
A Dio Void
Leafy Reefer
The Golly Dorm
Hello Bell
Flack Jackal
Lamb Canopy
Tinfoil Whip
The Lion Option
Pro Nose Job
Fail Root

Gazel Les
Jennifer Pageant
Prey Valet
When I Was the Writer
The Attach Emma
Developing Purse
The Attack Lag
Ratchet Progress
Detect Chest
Two Dollar Plum
Duke Bootleg
Baby Wise
Ad Lib Otter
Cute Whiff
Brutus Throughout
Clobber Stick
Bank Closer
The Hang Management
Purr Shorts
Pallid Lip
Greet Mason
Ripe House
Flash Knot
Swoosh Kook
Del Coattail
Collar Saw
A Sadder Rad
Tang Gimlet
Mike Drip
Glamour Van

Sap Chalice
Default Cow
Hence Minnie
Sedate Conversation
Previous Digs
Clench Plenty
100 Something
Oops Tulip
Evident Bent
Doughy Kids
Scream Needless
Nip Aggie
Ick Grizzle
Exploit Toy
Fizzard
Tune-Up Broom
Sue Use
Fib Benefit
Camera Lung
Thumb Justice
Group Willpower
Tether Pet
Yip Sis
The Yarn Chart
Come Pundits
Glib Reeker
Dim Pincer
Divorce Corn
Jabber Status
An Ann

When I Was the Writer

I remember a time when I wrote
something and gave it to a friend.
She must have read it because later
she said, "I read what you wrote."
This was a time when people wore
long red cloaks and all words were sung.
I was swaying but then suddenly
forgot the radio wasn't on. Puttering
was big in those days, too, so I puttered.
Again, this time, almost by accident,
I tried to write myself out of myself.
It was no fun, this poking and restarting.
But how else to solve the weird light?
I felt a droning shift as the bird moved
across the sun. I felt a twinge
of something almost robot.
But there was no red dot in the forest.
Even as cars turn corners, there
was no appeasing the gut.

Jess's Gesturing

Jess, behind the counter, motioned
at everyone, as if gesturing were completely
natural, as if it wouldn't eventually destroy
her, her home, her friends, her lovers, as if
it weren't responsible for the enslaved kids,
the ones driven by remote control, with
the steel in their gums. Her motions
were like swastika limbs, all dangling
through midair. The wildest of her gesturing
took the form of smallish wrist and hand
movements, as if holding invisible forks or
pistols or the strings to some wild puppet.
I often marveled at her brashness. The way
she would just flick her hand into the air within
close proximity of her body. She acted totally
normal, like this gesturing wouldn't solve
the mysteries of dark gemstones, like
all the mirrors in the world weren't turning
in their graves. Of course, I mean all of the dead
mirrors. The live mirrors aren't turning in their
graves but they are wincing, big time. I feel like
a glacier somewhere, sometimes. As if her
gesturing isn't real at all. Like we'll make it.
Like we'll all really make it.

Um Custom	After All This
The Clever Left	Different Goods
Bed Blessed	Critique Meat
Owing to the Unconscious	Nuance Amp
The More Sequence	The Common Stub
Overhead Who	All Rods
A Similar Vista	After Mass
Diverse Under	Danger Names
Outset Onset	To Devote Herself Entirely
Denim Hymn	The Must Offender
Super Medulla	Village Slit
Self Tempt	Ox Earwig
Socialist Pity	Quality Wilt
Precisely This	Jove Mugger
This Without Knowing	Five Sniper
Beg Feather	Blow Plow
Gimme Wimp	Con Fife
Disguise Iron	Jess's Gesturing
Mix Symbol	Nor Nietzsche
Sartre Darts	Regular Symptoms
The Bear Itself	The Other Type
Book Writers	Effect Wherefore
The Latter Criminal	Nervous Service
Profound Out	On the Way to Rome
The Motive Dolt	Caution Gown
Blame Sanctuary	Ill Teen
The Utter Constraints	Abundant Mud
Pull Wrongly	The Brittle Becoming
The Betray Cater	Rink Spirit
The Unfree Deep	Damp Land

The Acute Moody
The Had Battened
Strength V Strength
Regal Bleat
The Voice of
    Disappointment
Vine Leg Iron
The Heavy Mistrust
Terrible Rib
Drink Poison
Tug Gumption
Human Uni
Van Ramp
Clear Bus
Gifts for Others
Chill Genghis
Bits Superior
Fam Shape
Glisten Pills
Prompt Op
Loose Air
Lately Walleye
Juniper Blend
Cringe Carpool
Lace Oslo
Downtown Kite
Plummet Gun
Got Dot
Silent Vice
Presto Salt

Gold Balloons
The After Option
Dead Sea Scabs
Clad in Venus
Gill Digest
The Sheep Always
Group Riser
The Mall Blueprint
Anchors Not on Boats
Ivy Dig
Older Bulb
The Ski Beach
Back Scab
The Rehearsal Bourbon
Work Ill
Cat Hitch
The Anxiety Hangout
The Rowboat Matter
Dust Rudder
Pylon Goodbyes
The Kiss Whittle
Über Teleport
Echo Hole
White House Interns
Lament Opera
Feud Pot
A Bright Ray
Alien Pastries
Coy Prune
Nude Delude

Gash Goal	Maim Mob
Sherlock Moans	Moxie Toddy
Crumb Burt	The Conspire Lighthouse
Slower Load	Should Y'all
List Tiger	Dandering
Placard Robber	Shard Floss
Astro Pop	Got La La
Comet Net	Busy Inmates
Grin Swindle	Sun Acting
El Bib	Do Wilder
Swap Roger	Gloss Meters
Ringer Tone	Numb Earner
The Swells Up Nicely	Seizure Bee
Phase Haste	Foe Oak
Harp Lariat	Vigor Mitten
Boon to Cougar	Hit Hot
Guesser Mist	Guy Litany
Must Hinkly Oswald	Induce Oph
Pink Bear	Juke Kola
Goon Noggin	Nest Dink
Campground Twilight	Seven Month Tool
Mermaid Awesome	Suffer Uncle
The Somewhat Handbag	Philly Ilk
Frisk Nibbles	Neo Roofer
Talking About Practice	Tip Getter
Park Bullets	Twine Shine
Fantastic Applesauce	Future Ruth
The Done It Prow	Civil Liver
Unknown Hampton	Gruff Rug
Court Tacky	Lab Tuna

Hotel Smirk
The Wring Clean
March Pollster
Power Drought
Brutal Flute
Primo Shoe
Spruce Rue
Kidney Giver
The Dig Smidgen
Diner Ham
The Libby Blitz
Ore Corsage
Your Hand in Mine
Scavenger Mule
Riser Wobble
Happy Vat
Truth Muter
Geez Beacon
LA Renter
Subway Breath
Gender Squint
Droop Truce
A Perfectly Bandaged Thumb
Gershwin Curb
Slot Diablo
Probable Judo
Troop Juice
Tonight Owls
Blander Chant

Wince Cake
The Limp Gimmie
Boss Shank
Jab Badge
Timber Engine
Courage Ruse
Lake Grave
The Cry Idol
Merlot Curl
Chit Fat
Lubbock Rust
Mending Sin
Chance Seething
All Gall
Gumbo Lunch
Trill Fisher
Stress Guesses
Inch Beast
Gallon of Caffeine
Pleasure Egg
Faux Lummox
Gobble Bottle
The Meow Pout
Shudder Vermouth
Glove Triumph
Token Clop
Took Moo
The I've Migrant
Savior Waiver
Um Postal

Vase Candy
Banker Cows
Shifter Pill
Menacing Push
Ginger Pinup
Mingler
The Walls of Urk
Weak Me Too
Slacker House
Grinder Pro
Nil Acquit
Some Victory
Latitude Plot
Gone Straw
Honey Clot
Harp Pardon
Wool Lotus
Minnow Lens
Lotta Charlotte
Wing Twin
Corner Work
Cut Man
Drams of Lamplight
Could While
The Big Cubby
Gravity Sack
Satchel of Madness
The Glade Age
Baby Spore
Trés Klepto

Gladder Mass
Jefferson Claw
Front Dork
Plaid Sabbatical
Fink Ink
Slab Tabby
Shellshock Bot
Peer Grip
The Gondola Turn
Threat Pecker
Convene Either
The Mighty Chime
Odd Stagecraft
Drunk Breath
Ohio Grappler
Spurn Runner
Gum Thistle
Taxi Cheat
Skin Pinto
The Flick Kit
Truck Glutton
Void Boy
Club Schubert
Sledding Toward Vishnu
Jive Revival
Renew Tube
Local Trope
Plenty Sinner
The Tad Paddle
Vole Host

Lust Corpus
Grey Lately
Cap Passion
Doll Culture
Straddle Past
Born Crimper
Vacation Pager
Little Grendel
The Cobweb Step
Super Pretty Sister
Gird Underworld
Murk Journey
Vast Satchel
Blake's Wife
Core Dumbo
Sleep Fingers
Mall Keyword
Coif Moses
Am Panic
Assume Brood
Clues to Ruben
Shoot Duo
Oops Tulip
Graze Parade
Comma Tomboy
Spin Pit
Cad Pratfall
Gift Biscuit
Did Fiddle
Face Sample

The Bad Ladder
Crisp Through September
Candor Fan
Muffin Glut
Pride Finale
Shrink Grimace
Bid Dibs
Sin Nymph
All the Way to Dallas
Cliffs of Insanity
Boast After
Early Church Curse
Greaser Peep
Tweed Elbow
Ornery Tort
Piston Vision
See You in Pittsburgh
Owe Potion
Chair Sweetheart
My Busy Schedule
Only Fall
The Come On Let's Go
The Can I Watch
    Something
Awake Gift Shop
Jiffy Isn't
Hood Size
Telescope Hot
Carol Brady's Makeup
The Invention of Soups

Basic Petticoat
Bald Kids
Brick Christmas
Birth Other
City List
Seattle Middle
Operation Alice
Loose Chute
Pardon Lobby
Sog Gosling
Plutopia
Zen Miser
Ninja Limp
A Bower of Ladders
Cud Suckle
Love Bludgeon
Script Tea Party
The Noted Philanthropists
Lucky Cage
Tad Coward
First Tempter
Walled in Horses
Mud Recorder
Nib Nub
Quid Deal
Ali Mustache
Dig Killer
Apt Afro
Dead Bester
Side of White Shoes

The East Deed
Plenty Inseam
Head Hole
Blonde Convert
Prom Arbor
Zero Bid
Ivory Dealer
Star Lacquer
Modern Products
Coup Doer
Mink Bean
Intern Ticket
The Has Shasta
Bumper Clot
Pudding Table
Stitch Face
Dish Pear
Snatch Simpson
Puff Resort
For Instance Fleet
Ego Mission
Gold Helmet
Six O'clock Newsmen
Rose Uncommon
Ridge Commitment
Hardwire Bible
Occupy Notion
Insist Police
The Flashpoint of
  Discontent

Cars on Fire
Idiot Pigment
Horn-Rimmed Hate
Smolder Suit
Slum Variable
The Seduce Future
Freeze Commercial
Unjust Sport
Parish Looter
Reeling in Paris
Cave Nobody
Static Cyst
Autograph Hounds
Peck Bachelor
Flag Saddle
Agent Sofa
Thank You Slang
Knock Bull
Orange Wingtip
Principal Stunt
The Stop It Problem
Bad Fish
Booze Poodle
Cherry Rain
Leave It to Cleaver
Minister Bigger
Shy Right
The Now Piston
Evermore Regular
Noon Moon

The Forest Let Go
Felony Ella
Near Given
Bare Legs Besides
Dragged Thru the Woods
Clinic Entrance
Wind Demo
Volly Pedro
Widow's Beak
Crease Eater
Trust Pin
Sour Pout
Different-Sized Balloons
The Between Pinch
Certain Walls
The Second Third
Boat Tail
The Encumbered Journey
The If Whimper
Pitchfork So
Following the Cold
Brand Candle
The Rumored Divorce
Kidnap Past
Slum Fandom
Beginner Germ
Derby Boos
Tree Rigor
Mouse Plastic
Glimmer Quit

The Encumbered Journey

I was looking for the destination,
moving as unencumbered as nothing is
since everywhere in the world I see
encumbering. I was going to say, "The
snow! As unencumbered as the snow,"
but then I thought about gravity and
temperature and remembered the geometry
of living and then, poof! There went
the snow. I am thinking of birds now,
the way they seem to struggle
for a moment behind the foliage, as if
trapped in a stick cage, but then
break free. But they're encumbered
by the wings, the feathers, the blood—
just like the rest of us. So, there go
the birds. It's the destination, after all.
I'm not sure it matters who gets
there, how. The journey is for the past,
man, I'm talking about the future here,
where the lions raise their heads and
roar and the golden manes puff into
the air like they're singing some song.
But, it's not a song, it's the mane of
a lion and the lion beneath it is full
of fury and the road to forgiveness is

filled with fur that can't be petted.
It is in a zoo you might recognize but
be unable to enter. It's a sort of crab,
whose pinchers are hollow but whose
pinchers are vicious. It's a whole leg
of butchery but only one bone of hope.

Saucer Horizon
Morris Notebook
The Suspensioneers
Mince Wardrobe
Nice Rifle
Whale Taylor
Bison Kite
Blood Trumpet
Rio Key
Pre Creation
Thorn Dumpling
Thin Wild Noise
Cell Protocol
Weird Bunkmate
Sworn Newbie
Side Moose
Elope Mode
Robot Crime
More Torso
Uzi Pink
Far Car
Rooster Sum
Rhino Fire
Cope Post
The Crush Icing
Nil Bliss
Glue Pooch
The Yip Build
Also Wormhole
Use Cruise

Deuce Move
Clamper Lamb
New Uniforms
Get Whither
Zip Biz
Ply Ideal
Not Even on a Map
The Refuse Beauty
Suede Paper
Acting Like Children
Apology Hole
Festival Sweat Suit
Welcome to the Coup
Taper Grudge
Spy Worker
Behold Low!
Industry Belle
Veg Mesh
Carmel Soon
Hard Snail
Medium Scurvy
Nothing but Cable
A Kurt Loder Joke
Stalky Walk
Gone Guard
Senseless Bio
Correct Daylight
Vogue Stone
The Did Harkin
Think Rimbaud

Really Clear Head
Kitsch Across
Cinch Worthwhile
Queasy S
Straw And
Stomach Touché
Silent Eye
Doubt Port
Ordinance Dust
Kindred Vince
Hand Cuff Pun
Group Hula
The Kiss & Makeups
Gnat Millions
The Tower Strategy
Stagy Breakdown
Pound of Less
Age Hand
The Do Don't Now
*
The Commit Diff
Planning Manner
Swim Memo
Dino Jaws
Wool Luger
Plan Manor
Drum Murk
Goliath Cog
Ergo Preen
Landfiller

Crumb Rummy
Nudge Fiend
Silk Brothers' Bedtime
The Inclement Fringe
Porn Pelt
Duals with Congressmen
The Stuff Together
Catholic Fang
Standard Face Rake
Bag Baby
Overt Bird
A Lifetime of Pentagrams
Backmasking
Mid Curl Burst
The Janet Sandstorm
A Want Buy
Addict Film
Toll Free Wishes
Beige Rating
The Lived Inland
Mouse Faker
Blurry Hundred
Spring Filling
Eye Braces
Skip Hobby
Guitar Clock
Skinpire
Processed Dim
The Even Zoom
Cemetery Suite

¾ Sleeve T-Shirt
Chilly Vent
Earner Pal
Tidal Panda
Soap Whales
Biff Tit
Misused Feud
Village M's
Court 13
Genie Dent
Safe Cabbie
Escape DJ
The Gym Equipment
Phillip Reaper
Frugal Cupid
Golly Hardship
The Plane Midair
Dark Thirsty
Grunt Upper
Coliseum Magi
Host Motor
Comma Monetary
Loom Moose
Terse Purr
Womb Kidder
Lawyer Ow
Hair Parasol
Rain Brunet
Corridor Warp
The Right Mayo

Maiden Visage
Brian Lion
Yippy Mint
Boxer Clench
The Menudo Crushes
Gross Pen
Detergent Alone
Instinct Fight
Driver Vice
Croak Morning
Pace Revolution
Inside Down
Leverage Rest
Minute Uke
Toga Go For
Boa Jump Rope
Assembly Wine
Cabinet Offing
Bat Flip
The How Upset
Race of Hiccups
A Lesser Better
Bait Crater
Game Satan
Plush Ambush
Strike Zorro
Yesser Noer
Double Orphan
What Heather
Shortness of Death

Touched Lung
The Previous Free
Dearth of Gabors
Clean Pinky
Revel the Holy
The Exact Sources
Trans Subway
Lamb Camp
Flu Tutor
Prior Orbit
China Might
Bean Shimmy
Easy Being Hank
Tom Landry Middle School
Right Brown
Cluster Vern
An Ignorant Man
Bed of Leather
Quarry Drugs
Mint Papers
Random Acts of Whatnot
Farth Eirst
Fed Def
Towel Manger
Cuter Collar
Place Cutter
Closure Okay
Boom Cow
Dead Waiter
Easy Bingo

Bygone Class
Lift Kingdom
Hayward Fowl
The Exceed Bead
The New Better
Central Intel
Fid Get
Ghost Rosin
The Trickle Downs
Beach Cub
Free Score
Seat Dime
Prop Het
Born Cape
Cole Slaw Station
Col. Ruble
Veil Lifter
Mum August
The Premier of Wisdom
Sis's Pot
Mamba Con
Neglecterine
The Mop Per
Bed Pill
Extra Spine
The New Downtown
Deals for Childhood
Pin Thin
Blank Nary
Fume Cuter

The Dig Quip
Fido Heart
Cough Fee
Early Pipedream
Avider Id
The Into Creaser
Pica Kid
Watt Luck
Fine Sturgeon
Zoo Cushion
Bus Pistol
Gust Summer
Juice Coolant
Stupor Flow
Decent Ender
Fist Cheap
Push Ever
Glass Snowplow
Who Shot Jay Are
Dirt Earner
Swan LeBron
Turn Umber
Shin Length and Yellow
Deem Hubris
Swear Pasture
Concussion Sandwich
Sled Prego
Pocket Combs
Hoot Fusion
Lava Aquatic

Work Watchers
Owl Dolly
Um Illuminati
Delta Socks
Your Job Ramirez
Pangifesto
The Boss of You
Headband Ban
Rent Krypton
Mesh Delaware
Groom Moor
Cognac Heart
Sorry Offer
Ernest Hurry
Bench Cinder
Nervous Judge
Prolapsed Adder
Le What Fern
Yell Ghetto
Getting Burlap
Anything Beep
Astro Pallet
Nor Avery
The Bail Lab
Carton Shard
Gal Talon
Saul of Walrus
The Divided I
The Ain't Crank
Vaster Plaid

Cain Undershirt
Blonde Zombie
Chess Bomb
Tomb Spoon
Bro Cobra
Hospital Tea
Fly Splat
The Editor Walter
Nun Onion
Under Humdrum
The New Wynton
High by Isaac
Milk Panties
Finger Toes
Platter As Is
Dude Movie
Latex Issue
The Racer Phase
Bathroom Drink
Leaf Meal
Solid Knob
The Flowers in Darkness
The Give Pivot
Lucian Boost
Den Shovel
The Alter George
Clair Various
Tie Spider
Past as Monologue
The Upper Fix

Tar Garden
Gold Plumbing
Tore Merchant
Verses in the Airmail
Base Pomegranate
Groan Porch
Boot Tool
The Ignore Sort
Grim Minnesota
The Pint Sign
Voyage Through the
   End Times
Jalopy Pincer
Coat Holder
Jank Haircut
Zero Cellular
Caleb Able
Tinkling Sink
Bleed Cesar
Core Bundle
Sin Iteration
Son Boast
Finch God
Mice Bylaws
Leader Pace
The Hormonal Component
Princess Diana's Wedding
The Warhol Globe
Dipolar Bisorder
Gaunt Lumber

Upset Tum Tum
Phony Accentia
Pharaoh Tote
Face Kitten
Milk Booth
Mouth Birdie
Fool Moon
Yo Feather
Cheese Breeze
Sticky Rock
Be There Margarine
Cool Landladies
Showstopper Op-Ed
Ha Crock
Animal Pie
About Squire
Tiger Guile
Femme in Knits
Quayle Potato
Terror in Orlando
The Evolution of Barnacles
Ape Kinship
Actual Howler
Massacre Class
Terror Ferry
Tal Low
Again Street
Iliad Beard
The Wife Tried
Gay Dater

Confirmed Goner
The Reporters in
    Washington
The Complete Ditto
Us Divide
Three B-Sides
The So Much Armor
The Evil Media
Employment Doily
Faster Jails
Tick and Sired
The Nightclub Packed
The Junior High Love Lives
El Quickest
The Yes Wait
The Laws in California
Liable Juice
Citizen Sit Down
The We Will
Get Down Bitch
Worst Cops Ever
Let Gost
Wheel Misery
Never Albania
Home Title
Larger Hardhat
O. J. Psycho
Candle Steamer
College Fry
More Bayonets

Slim Income
Pug Suspect
Drab Plates
Truck Wood
This Error
The Twelve Ratio
The Former Uppercase
The Fail to Mention
Radiocarbon Mace
Somewhat Plumper
No Other Nearby
Instead Livestock
Either Fish
Finally Taboo
Minor Crop
Hence We Ask
Piecemeal Trinity
Sheep Cereal
Pose Vacuum
The Added Certain
Another Been
The Mind and the Body
The Guide Themselves
Cider Plant
Humid Pea
Lousy Berries
The Species Fewer
The More Numerous Birds
Such Thrush
What We Call Farming

The Ready Size
The Inevitable Fruit
Color Seed
Amid Merely
Reason Eater
The Only Biggest
The Size of Bats
Spill En Route
Mango Before
Cyanide Dad
An Exceptional Degree
The Textile Supplier
Wild Squashes
The Occasional Acorn
Yam Roots
The Starve Offer
However Topical
Whereas Cannibals
Peon Web
The First Cereals
The Sweating Sickness
Single Nigeria
To Kill Fewer Rabbits
The Virus Outright
The Did Pathogen
Longer Before Dying
Example Fleas
Future Chief
Mono Polo
Effective B. C. E.

The Mind and the Body

The main issue is how the mind feels
separate from the body, how it imagines
itself both inside and outside of the body.
Of course the body doesn't like this
since, it says, "There is no inside or outside
there is only me." So they're sort of at
an impasse over that very basic point.
The mind can be a real jerk but the
body keeps going the whole time anyway.
Or it doesn't keep going, but we're not
discussing death and even if we were,
that's a good example of where the problem
is. The mind says, "I may be able to escape
death." But I don't think the body feels
like that. The body feels like death is a big
part of who it is. So, the body feels
underappreciated and the mind feels like
the body is a big baby for not conquering
death, but of course, the mind knows it
hasn't conquered anything either. It's
just a big game. The body thinks the mind
is crazy for not embracing death. And the
mind is crazy.

The Use of Youth

How cozy was the idea that we
would meet easily, nodding to each
other as we settle down. How sweet
the thought that we'd produce
flowers in our pockets, grow roses
under our arms. I knew even then
the covered bridge on the way
to church wouldn't be there forever.
That's why it was so important
that we made out in the darkness,
in basements, in cars with the radio
on. What's the use of youth if it
can't be spooned with your tongue?
What's the point of having your own
zippers if nobody ever unzips you?
In the stars we swallowed was the
light being let in from the hallway.
Our parents coming down stairs
was the noise that came with the
alarm in our hearts. Our hiccup
of kisses, a small bee.

Buttress Wingnut
Wide Skateboard
The Plow Conquest
The Exact Beer
The Empire Throughout
Urban Vest
The Use of Youth
The You'll See Saturn
The Camera Version
Crispy Nurse
Brick Whistler
Hail Thumb
The Library Mess
A Gimme Ending
Ozzie God
Chemical Boot
Sky Whitney
As Polite As
Piano Goose
Revelator Say
Broom Ooze
Communion Mustard
Early Surfer Man
Destroyer of Whirls
Lobe Oboe
Collector Wick
Clot Savvy
Bent Ending
Burn Worm
Gobs of Gifts

One Coma
Feet Like Roller Skates
Malt Drawl
The Incise Judo
The Power Moby
Nano Nana
Do Nar Leo
Flag Arbiter
The Dumps No One
Cameron's Apologetics
Call Zipper
A Bedtime Tantrum
Good London
Janky Dahmer
The Pet R. Arch
Diffidenter
The Orwell Or
Atta Wanda
Rogue Ovid
Laugh Eagle
The Lose Faith Babies
Immune Noon
Fashionable Suburbs
The Ain't Over Yes
Most of the Right Things
Transcript Pity
The Go-Between Egos
The Restraint Depot
Empty Tenure
Ever More Lesser

Only the Debris
The Elapsed Early
The Immediate Causes
Replaced Speakers
The Me Upheaval
Our Recent Misery
All Hauler
Media Eater
Surer Jury
Citing Mighty
Tame Gimme
Glacier Ploy
Did Conspiracy
Police Jesus
Remiss Its
Well Key
The Karate Montage
Moot Curio
Olive Slob
Murder Nut
Kick Widow
Evil Newton
Tux Bleach
When Hair Is a Weapon
Vacation Stomach
Once Under
Food Production
Lamé Scapegoat
The And/Or Lion
Rhine Stoner

Lotta Sexpot
The I Know Bogart
Heather Cigarettes
Lucian Cue Card
Sling Kinky
Feud Deputy
Cellar Bedpan
Rolling in Don't
Clamor Handprint
Enter Mistress
Clue Rudolph
Juice Format
Glib Filibuster
Panoply Pants
Tattoos in the 70s
Oscar Bottle
The Ridge Edge
Snarl Garage
Cabinet Glue
Name Thrower
Compute Mew
Card Boar
Flower Ado
Solomon Blockhead
The Went Consequence
The Rad Swaddle
Carwash Lass
Nettle Lever
Bazooka Kook
Sillar of Palt

Claymation Frustration
Eh Bee
Woe Betide
The Regime Under
Hollow Michigan
Fond Microbes
The Instead Decimate
His Beautiful Life
Middle Disease
Timid Man
The Biggest Killers of
   People
Heavy Gobble
Inordinate Few
Whooping Loft
Raw Brains
But Rabies
Hookworm Skin
Fat Consolation
Cannibal Heritage
Broadcast Germ
Favor Cloud
Victim Feces
The Never Mind Motives
An Ethical Pose
Suitable Host
The Most Vigorous Yet
Hence Frenzy
Cattle Glob
Feather Tent

The Pathogen Forward
The Sign for Bread
Obvious Arrow
Led Via Reverse
Fixed Sequins
Idea Diffusion
User Help
Five Twice
Hill Flower
Myth Different
Wine Jug
Nine Coils
Hiccup Disc
Inch Chin
Militant Pill
The Pie Tirade
Perchance Handy
Gift Quiver
Chez Hex
Mogo Pump
Crass Ascot
Devise Edison
The Suitable Limit
Firebomb Alchemist
The Who Tinker
Fund Bummer
Oil Lamb
The Hard Adopt
The Reject Yep
Dwindle Twins

Star Hardware
Ether Deer
The Empty Rich
The Nixon Switch
Blow Dish
Vigor Lids
Dick Kid
Miles of Lies
Lent Ender
Name Panky
Him Chime
The Dirty Hurry
Shimmy Into
Leather Checkbook
Let Goad
Still Willow
Smiter
Hostile Awk
Heck Chest
Pete Steep
The Majestic Get
Said Dias
Sleep Ace
The July Vice
Blood Sundress
Loose Druid
Clue Juniper
Soil Boon
The As Is Blast
Ice Mice

Bulb Cult
The Somewhat Voluptuous
Mass Carcasses
Manifest Disney
The Clearly Ruthful
Midst Maidens
The Few Legible
Thunder Tongue
Apocryphal Joshua
The Beasts of the Earth
Wolf Pie
The Spirit of Dead Women
Heavy on the Luminous
Red Bind
Newsroom Ooo
Exodus Lust
Word Flock
Perfect Minus
Off Wing
The Beget Giants
400 Feet Higher
The Exact Contents
Soap Lips
Waning Gate
The Among None
Wine Icy
Equal Lastly
Proceed Seed
Best Exit
To Avoid Levi

The Astonish Proper
Spliff Eager
Prelim End
Solar God
Comely Runt
Erasership
The Rest Disowned
The Better Trombone
Temple Nibble
Done Solid
Part Tarp
Glum Communist
Truce Cougar
Off Father
Quill Bill
Statue Fruit
The Size of Harlem
Soon Goose
The Guilty Feelings
Publishing Choke
Unfit Plum
The Garble Equines
Chamber Underling
Eel Quilt
Ham Battle
Sin Sling
Shoe Stones
The Newt Get
Blackbird Work
Porous Wig

The Keel Beneath
The Slightly Swigs
Apprentice Unending
Cab Tail
Vial of High School
Detention Time
The Hurt Suck
Grudge Trundle
Tool Loop
Vegas Stepchild
Clarity Islow
The Annoy Goat
Quibble Bigly
Woeful Primping
Clues Like Bloody Anvils
Glider Foot
Rube Coolant
In Cool Mud
The Cry Testify
The Assistant Imprint
Fairness Knife
New Jugular
The Old One Glove
Spoken Mermaid
The Telephone State
Sleet Creation
Credit Werewolf
Bag of Hate Mail
Billy Carter T-Shirt
The Cast of Mash

Weave Shapers
Fortunate Erstwhile
Damp Situation
Serious War
Raw Wagon
Tiny Eye Chart
Merge Curtain
Sledge Devil
Stalker Texas Danger
Glass Femur
Bike Totes
Succeeding in America
The Distant Path
Sixty Leagues' Distance
Uruk Elder
Cedar Forest
The Whom Burlap
Cluster Speech
Damsel Ignition
Proper Robbers
Wuss Overcoat
Bullet Orwell
Dead Greg
Wild Cow
Slander Bread
Neck Wings
Slew the Ogre
Smote Thicket
Auras Later
Two Afar

Choose Timber
The Tremble Hillside
Sixty Cubits
Take Hold Dove
Prewar Dump
The Rouse Crown
Me Seized
The Devour Cloth
Make Flesher
Hue Scooter
Boo Weakly
Chest Urchin
Serious Humdrum
Cleft Register
Sister Realtor
Pie Coyote
Red Foreskin
Motor Bicker
Sound Umpteen
Baby Vaccine
Three Ply Rope
Fellow Able
Combat Ox
Torry Spelllling Beee
Jade Shampoo
Good Frosting
Stoop Mother
Skirt Fire
The More Explode
Brat Legroom

Succeeding in America

It is not as if I can capture the high road simply
by mowing everyone down at the ankles. In fact,
as I try to navigate the crust, I find my desire
to spring forward is held in check my desire
to fall back. It's like, for each and every Newton
there is an opposite Newton, say, a fig, a Wayne
who is chubby as a tween but a real fucker
on the banjo. Also, as far as showmanship goes,
it's hard to beat a drum harder than all the
daydreaming eyes at the soda fountain or all
the twinkling cheeks at the record store. For
every black button on a lapel, there is a tiny wish
in my heart. At every hopeful talent show
the number of dance steps is the same number
of steps to my bed. In my bed, where my dreams
are cartoon surfers, I can feel the musing of
the future. I feel the skin that isn't yours spread
across an ocean that isn't ours. It's like the foam
in my throat is a bubbled snake, like the vest
in my chest is a fur grenade.

The Dainty Ninjas

They are more beautiful and
predictable than the massive
ninjas, who are not predictable
or beautiful, but like wisps
of horse hair, you find them
in your imagination, stirred
in a past silent sauce.
My advice isn't very helpful
but I'd advise you to get
help somewhere. The dainty
ninjas, like boarded-up ghosts,
each hop on one foot, trying
to see the thunderstorm.
These ninjas aren't powerful
but they are merciful, like
a god that no religion has
discovered yet.

Used Soup
The Hey Man Blanket
Clogs Named Robert
The Inverse Worse
Thumb Bunt
Deli Cheeses
Eve Freed
The Clean Least
Bull Gull
Makeshift Kin
True Jupiter
Pander Camera
Greed Cleats
Kitchen Shoes
Vo Cremate
Women in the Media
Honey Plate
Decent Grease
Rather Ossified
Aqua Moss
A Screwup Beast
Lead Sawed Off
Push Ordinate
Heaven Bull
In Case There's Rubble
The Astonish Honor
Sorrow Tomorrow
A Nearly Impossible Lifetime
Cube User

The Killers Out There
Rich Gidget
Fillet Basin
Civil Leaf
Briefer Siblings
Short Charring
The Eye Hustle
Husk Other
By Chance Humble
With Isn't
Computers Made of Bark
The Peered At
Harlot Ale
Seven Goblets
Hi-Tech Door Knocker
Sore Rosary
Edify Head
Jail Roulette
Well Done Dog
The Arrest Pheasant
Cats Named Lucifer
Chill Schism
The Dainty Ninjas
Ester Celebration
Dumb Luncheon
Brim with Mirrors
Corpse Down
Police Without Warrants
Picked Daisies
Whiner Likely

Pilfer Will
Old Oranges
Spring Prosperity
Creepy Pipe Organ
Lovers Collecting
Worker Must
A Childhood of Scrap Wood
Railway Harmonicas
Earn Front
Cabinet Now
Clear into Summertime
Burp Parson
Dagger Badminton
Milk Shook
Shrill Lettermen
Preluder Fruit
One Sock Shower
Villain Lean-To
The Tiff Menu
Robe Throat
Bud Hoops
Fellow Dose
End In
Coo Lather
The Ran Forward Always
Rush Hour Suicide
Pen Infant
Incidental Sven
Hester Preen
Kid Nap Pan

Corner Lung
Puncture Dimsdale
Drawing Bridget
Clean Soaker
Cornice Imp
Whoa Brother
Green Broom
Simmer Bella
The Rotate Laces
Gent Ting
Moss Atom
Poni Pony Pone
The Gee Lynx
The Nervous Vroom
Teflon Donnybrook
A Whole Lot of Rooster
Cherry Lamp
Quid Amigo
Zamboni Ham
Star Marvin
Mega Off
Blink End
Pew Furious
Hotplate Fiesta
Mooch Heart
Scoot Kitty
Ointment Pig
Slather Aptly
Thin Minute
Youth Tunisia

O Shrub
Android Pants
Etch Fielder
Dark the Or
Grown Photons
Yelp Pinto
Bake Nook
Pear Earrings
Drug Skill
Earlier Skulls
Ton Pomp
Skinny Forensic
The Jillion Pill
Podunk Rum
Dial Violation
Skid Wardens
Cash for Organs
Pie Winner
Reef Pylon
Cutting Down Trees
Karma Armada
Rule Urbana
Marquee Ouster
Peach Crewcut
Super Paper Umbrellas
Breathe Tournament
Blah Caveat
Frampton Math
Gland Antler
These Accursed Modern
    Times

Spectral Art
Against Moser
Extremely Careful
    Movements
An Infinity of Times
Maestro Obey
Velvet Waistcoat
Arc Star
Glossy Fast
Stout Man
Laden Tables
Pickled Bone
Rocket Paperwork
Born Anyone
Sniffler
Drama Pond
Freedom Tack
Kid Tick
Check Sport Coat
Reaper Needs
Grip Itsy
Mama Pawn
Doctor Quietly
Flat Wallet
Charm Dolly
Vague Bigness
Stave Offer
Slick Gym Floor
The Know Because
Eek Secret

Shallow Guy
Guile Paradigm
Tongue Thunder
Albeit Treason
Too Sooty
Shooting Bye-Bye
Freeload Go Boat
Historic Rigmarole
Home Moran
Stuffed Onion
Tempting Meow
Tremor Wren
The Gleam Meter
Chin Scab
Glass Icing
Hike Silence
Nary a Brief Shadow
Host Pom-Pom
Deli Kate
Vicarious Lesbos
The Mirth Version
Champion Hot Sauce
Studio Eve
Felix Heartthrobber
Clap Tots
Dang Veggies
Merlin Honing
Freckle Legs
Topic as Such
Flesh Edie

Moon Bike
Universe Hood
Cook Lozenge
Styles of Lying
Thrum Money
Loser Purvey
The Gotten Chart
The Very Noose
A Tired Pie Thief
Flame Rowboat
Space Cluster
Coal Lotus
The Fast After
Lewd Jeweler
The Um Fume
Hyper Exile
Drill Vicar
The Someone Thorn
The Interrupt Teen
Soakering
Tomorrow Bandy
Thin Rings
Modern Roger
Skive Finch
Bored with Therapy
Aisle Sweetheart
Leah Virgin
The Keeps It
Giles Bonnet
Under Punt

Chosen by Moses
Rear Deathbed
Shovel Bug
Girl Lotion
Portal Orchid
Goading Goliath
Mass Password
The Awhile Vice
Vegan Teeth
Knuckle Rosary
Oboe Probe
Western Robin
Fraud Forum
Deal Whisker
Past Caverns
Goth Moth
Your Own Polling
Rescue Mutt
Dug Florence
Ezekiel Feeder
The Plenty Empty
Light Waver
The Running from
    Vampires
Bed Kettle
Dune Muggy
The Instead Options
Even Newer Proof
Two Fingers of Scotch
Tinge Numbers

The Upper Slum
The Face of Young Chess
Dance Caper
Thirty Questions or So
Fad Cadaver
Ash Pasture
Even String
Bloom Movement
The Tried Fighting
Swan Wand
Splat Pattern
Enter Vic
Bipolar Lip
The Tenth Mention
Hush Doesn't
Corner Ordinate
Hair Fan
Strange Tux
Feeler Chain
Shy Dresser
DDDDDDD
Pluck Negotiation
Our Embarrassing Past
Gin Cheeks
Posit Dimples
The Cold Homeless
The Colossal Nag
Blob Transfer
Hot Trotter
The Heather Horn

Loyal Sweatshop
Cigar Fox
Loud Brow
Reparation Payday
Vintage Squid
Window Fern
The Share Knot
Bike Chain
Camp Slander
Nap Mishap
Quinn Grass
Gut Dud
User Tube
Rooster Loot
A Significant Lather
Low Stroke
Closer Depot
Pagan Dread
The Birth Hornet
Sluice Foot
Your Coke Robe
Loon Otter
The Grave Stage
Lone Punman
Mad Javelin
Crow Sweater
The Get Neatly
Chess Elephants
Honey Glue
Baby Case

The Solution Fool
Floral Industrial Complex
Darn Carnations
The Total Two Steps
Dinner Sweatpants
The Available You
Bawler Face
Milk Gutter
Dude Pew
Some Lungfish
Mule Cutie
Organ Doorstop
Dragon Gun
The Funnier Fake
Sober Days
A Greater Famine
Starter Auger
Bumble Gunk
Nice Hair Dryer
Prosthetic Torso
Kid Patter
Cub Truster
The Cad Knack
Panda Lance
Strewn Lucian
Blister Key
Of the Mountain
The Fifth Rib
The Yet to Cry King
But Jezebel

Breach Priest	A Threesome Feat
The Arose Grove	City Pump
The Dwelt Deed	Stalk Alter
Sixteen According	Glam Mailroom
Goose Food	Surf Perfect O
Wherefore Fowl	Yarn Pack
Meat Keith	Dirt Whale
The As-Good God	Dawn Garage
Dark Star Visor	Sham Pancakes
Kingdom Shimmy	Mid Why
Damnation Lamb	The Miss Technician
Blaspheme Photon	Early Roman Sculpture
Salt Booty	Drone Farewell
Drinking Vice	Um Momentum
The Us Supper	Bony Roof
Nude Judas	The Top Thirty
Fed Bird	Strobe Road
Clay Abrahams	Checkers to Kick Around
The Fisher Coats	Chug Nut
The Ergo Thirst	Hog Grout
Linen Middle	Black Plastic Bag
Rise Again Must	Genie Pants
Trunk Full of Sisyphus	Outgoing Box
Goliath Turbine	Wimp Machine
Baptist Lad	Bun Hunt
The Understood Not	Little Sybil
One-Third Moses	Clue Tourniquet
The Hard Barter	Carbon Floppy
Foe Abode	Tool Boot
Lover Bomb	Cook County Marriage

War Shop
Elevator Pelt
Fizzery
Lead Boomerang
Cred Prob
Pest Soda
Beaten Fruit
Rot Gnats
Florida Burning
Nub Bunny
Thumb Biter
Store Boar
Glue Pool
Day Glow Phase
Few Phantoms
Obliging Ghost
Smokey Establishment
Arch Pawn
Liqueur Kin
Narrow Fanatic
Resort Daughter
Vexed Western
Convenient Fever
Ditch Softly
Animated Family
The Proven Useful
Bone Buttons
Black Sea Patch
Clockwork Train
Risk Fit

Else Jabbed
Lick Circus
Lending Den
The Future as We Planned It
The Often Crib
Alien Cheatsheet
Words for Vermin
Chimp Simpsons
Ze Busy Bodiezzzz
Newborn Lapels
The Forbid Rug
Bear Hanging
Yellow Phonograph
Fat Janitor
Halt Hats
The As-If Master
Youth Tutor
Ick Picnic
Mother Duck
The Related Despair
Good Fission
Joke Cornet
The Daring Middle
Apple Gag
Hemlock Massage
Miniseries Villain
The Beverly Revelations
Nosebleed Heart
Blonde Condo

The Future as We Planned It

"Don't blow the tube larger than it
needs to be," she warned, but I was
in no mood for warnings
and so I blew the tube far larger
than was necessary. And that was
the least of my flubs. I fucked
up the stuff in the cupboard, too.
In those days I was a mess.
But when she arrived with the code,
the dictation, and the system,
I wasn't prepared at all. I remember
standing in the doorway, in my plastic
suit, pulling the hood over my ears,
fixing my eyes on the corner.
In the wide open, everyone could
sense the future. I had doubts, but
told no one. The warnings continued
and by spring, most of us were
weaving through the fields
and aluminum bleachers.
The rose that no one wanted to grow
began blooming by the school.
The nun that no one wanted to hear
began growling in the choir.
When the winter was thinking of

pulling off autumn's skirt, the bad boy
inside of me gave way. I no longer
listened when the voice started.
In a way, I was oblivious. In another
way, I was a murderer whose
crimes just hadn't happened yet.

The Thurston Burn
The Midst of Greatness
The End Potential
Omni Egg
Hen Power
Weasel Feast
Loose Muse
A Jillion Handprints
Shiver Fig
Sage Grenade
Pier to Venus
Hell Munch
Pocket Dot
Pillow Grill
Mess Vessel
El Weepo
Modeling School
Wet Cur
The Simple Crocodile
Bird Tattoos
The Present Edge
Empty Gallons
Round Hut
Muddy Sun
Clay Veil
Earth Cake
Springtime Killers
Basic Jason
Overdose Animal
Rainbow Satan

Throat Corn
Zebras Bleed Too
The Bitch Primitives
Kevlar Sailboat
The Minus Billy Ocean
Famous Handles
Clinging to Gym Shorts
Saber Railway
Cage Man
Minnie Thumbs
Hellcat Sweater
Ryan Scion
Nice Pie
Neither Greener
Ream Deacon
Rotation Goals
A Plan for the Average
   American
The Deli Roar
Parts of the Equation
Shale Raincoat
A Plan to Meet the Parents
Celebrity Spinach
The Doomed Fur Trade
Yolo Halo
Crepe Yeses
Ghouls Named Susan
Cave Maker
Sam Camo
Fink Benchmark

Shammer
The Creek's Weak Spot
Wine Slice
Sour Outage
The Yawn Encore
Gabor Sweatband
Thrice Rhino
Gaff Tadpole
Rib Web
Fad Clef Note
Days Without Accidents
Normal Accents
Syringe Dustpan
The Sleeping Bag Zippers
Octopus Room
The Homework Policy
Gam Channel
Pew Polish
Omnipotent Pinup
The Waddle Won't
Banana Cramps
The Postcard Museum
Air Mare
Full Fledged Jethro
Foist Orb
Hitler's Mustache
State of Gravy
Ruthlessly Yours
Senator Bigmouth
Mao Gift Basket

Chain Light Wave
Born Ornery
Slop Rapture
Machine Pun
Boxed Possum
Free to Please
Roar Womb
Champ Dander
Fixed Id
Courage Vader
Ethic Cleansing
Scrubbed White Library
Boss Longitude
Big Rig Summer
The Ghastly Hourglass
Shale Turnip
Early Checkmate
Square Earth
Yum Funnel
Nero Fiddle
Moses Flub
Itty Fidget
Hawk Elbow
The Willpower Outhouse
Shooting Sprain
Grow Brother
Crass Past
The Tersely Worded Email
Lincoln Not Well
Normal Porn

Posters of Roses
Led Woodshed
Well Short Cord
Blare Air
Savage Heir
Sad Algebra
Dapper Paw
Dirt Purchaser
White Blood Cellular
Crossword Pervert
Boot Crooner
Scab Badge
Pony Made of Satan
The Unearth Dijon
Suicidal Encyclopedia
Mint Well
Hundreds of Thumbs
The Flair Liars
Bed Ketchup
Clean Vent
Trashed Mass
A Case of Bottled Hot Sauce
The Ides of Crucify
Fork Berry
Willow Till
Glare Heirloom
Queer Barber
Grandmother Buzz
Special Types of Shoes
Of With About Around And

Looking at Me Directly
Keg Rumpus
The Lawn Dart Epoch
Clair Low Waist
Snaz Plaza
Leotard Spring
Shadow Fan
Pee Soup
Even Creases
Pleather Radios
Famous Gold
Soul Garment
The Wrong Weird Crystal
A Page from Get Better
Cellar Pay Phone
An Uncertain Ruin
Lunch Busking
The Vibe Hybrid
Beautiful Fencer
Chooser Wolves
The Cool New Lou
Hot Tub Cologne
The O My Body Paint
Rule Jewelry
The Serious Crewmen
Cosmetic Head
Villa Names
Tusk Oven
Land Planner
Loop Pool

Actors in the 1960s
New York Pity
Cloven Robots
Hearse Budget
Gruesome Toad
Ode Riverboat
Pill Teardrop
Rain Gumshoe
Uzi Extra
The Road Returning
Suits Full of Rich Meat
Skimpy Cuba
The Root of All Eagles
Avenging Velvet
Skipping the Previews
A Hole to Fill
Bum Sternum
Deny Any
Widower Pin
Kung Foot
Snug Scalp
Future Us
Surplus of Foot Rubs
Prozac Vat
I've Frightened
We Go Fort
Bubble Wrap Poppers
Been Ninja Fooled
Astro Woman
Normal Stunt

Inch Pincher
Picket Hence
Rotten Horse
Syrup Whiskers
Clever Bedfellow
Paper Grape
Function Uncle
The Incorporated Say
Very Much That Much
My Wife the Engineer
Model Stare
Breakdown Saver
Adopt-a-Pet
Father of the Yearly
Cheek Yo
Ran Through
The Memories of the University
Yeti Asia
Large Scale Pastry
Random Galumph
Nun Box
Bit Zipping
Booze Corkscrew
Dead Hair
Fire Wife
Kid Trigger
Hobo Beans
Wet Backseat
Piranha Hose

Tinier Mice
League of Fruit Trees
Quantum Eggplant
Politicians in Sweatsuits
Clues to Rhubarb
Supper Eyes
Nose Bud
Goat Hoax
Stint in Juvie
Pear Hysteria
Rapt Has-Been
Aft Badger
Lap Tick
Delay Babe
Bladder Scab
Show Pinto
Flag Garnet
The Pacific Get
The Frugal Pull
Stern Thanks
Opportune Scurry
Zoot Tool
Cleaver Beast
Gleam Meanness
Spy Vitals
The Swindle Gene
Outline Sampson
Oops Scoop
X-Ray New Yorkers
Snuff Shuttle

Trauma Savant
Shun Dump
Houses Like Blue Pies
Disco Tape
Brain Downside
Head Fang
Scene Wing
Long Black Coattails
Stick Figurers
Harm Arbor
Staple Acorns
First Ticket
Cartoon Maids
Big Nose
Florida Rest Stop
Q Dips
Gold Nolan
The Campus Pants
Loll Wool
The Obsessed Ex-Lovers
Hag All
Hater Maid
Pasted Cape
Warning Plot
Feather Lips
If Shifter
Bleat Geezer
Foam Cyborg
Let Requester
Hannibal Vantage

Chin Administer
Fierce Ear
Sin Glen
Positive Ants
Money Comb
New Lice
Hunce Dat
Outer Gases
Yes Bedlam
College Preppy
Nit Mop
My Love for You
Sob Call
Either Speed
Victim Pretty
Sweet Pug
Grave Cake
Dead Lizard
Less Fresno
Swarm Armor
Plastic Bag
Said Bedpost
Stilt Willard
The Pummel Happening
Square Dance
The Uphill Cusp
The Skate Faithful
Bully Puncher
Siamese Samurai
Happening Sweetheart

The Long Trouser Crowd
What Todd Wrought
Night Ice Cream
Half Calf
Video Beef
Ipso Fizz
Cool Medulla
Melon Pelt
Eerie Peers
Brit Knickers
Slang Manger
Out of Frost
Mid Hickey
Old Liver Franklin
Sleepy Money Dupree
Big Legs Lee
The Repurpose Capacity
The Actually Heard Us
We're Out
Etch Reflex
Safety Mutt
Warsaw Seaweed
11,000 Death Threats
Plural Ernest
Force Fielder
Treason Vita
Wedge Codex
Stoop Poodles
Why Fireworks
Hard Gardner

My Love for You

It would slip the sleeping pill under your tongue.
—Jennifer L. Knox

First you feel a sort of nagging in your knees,
like a curly bug is crawling up your leg.
Before you can swipe it away, it's gone, cast backward
into the wind like the look on Lot's wife's face.
Speaking of salt, my love jumps through
the flavor of your dinner and impresses you
with the tanginess of sorrow.
When you want to open up and swallow,
it turns out you can't connect the food to your piehole.
Everyone's piehole is someplace different.
For instance, mine is in my hand and when I
wave I'm showing the world where I
load the insides. During a handshake, my lips
are closed but the moment I let go, they open
into a scream that sounds a lot like a tired
vacuum cleaner. I wish my love were better
but it's worse. I'm like a prince who turns
into a frog. Or, rather, like a prince who
isn't a prince or a frog, just some local hick
who's finally come around to the big cities
of Shit Sucks and O Fuck. Where the national
anthem is "I've Fallen and I Can't Get Up."

The Winner

It was because I didn't
believe in the supernatural.
It was because everyone
is doomed to be silly
sometimes. Of all the tall
apostles in the world,
I stand so tall it's lonely.
Exposed, as if in a roomy
park, with wide meadows
and a brook swishing by,
open to the weather like
a fur-covered animal or the
open waters of the ocean.
In that space in time there
is a drawing on a wall,
a ship that sinks behind
the clouds, a cascading
sort of sensation, a sort
of tingle that might represent
a gulf in time or the pattern
in the jacket a prophet wears.
All through a war there is
a winner, it's just nobody
knows who it is yet.

Cheater Fleece
Galloping Goddess
Beer Prisoner
The Dodder Forward
Extinct Sunfish
Golly Bod
Trip to Rio
Doorbell Speedo
Sinking Tristan
Revenge Fringe
Salmon Knee
Old Poll
Narrow Pie
The Winner
Dinky Fink
Brown Awe
Kepler Bellow
Nap Matter
Bag Full of Almost
Sullen Creep
Weekly Miss
Juice Tree
Skid Ding
Regular Vestibule
Meddling Dids
Boy Overjoyed
Cinder End
Chimney Wimp
Goal Bowl
Aught God

Family Stampede
Work Cork
Amen Hater
Flower Saboteur
The Shan't
Owl Lasso
Chilly Peach
Step Dead
Scald Mall
Little Astronaut
Pledged Renoir
Gretchen Retch
No Pie
Flack as Such
Beautiful Shortstop
Mickey Ick
Grub Boner
One Common Goat
Yip Digger
Tongs for Oswald
Deaf Heaven
Gang Rainbows
Defiance Style
What Hawk
Lightweight Heavy
Goatee Chat
Gall Cauldron
Batshit Cashcow
Do Good Pluto
Mile Fairly

Rude Freud
Ditto Dada
Oiler Hopes
Love Mortgage
Goal Sausage
The Lion Warship
Originally February
Clause Gull
Bent Star
Parables of Worship
Silt Penny
The Scars of Woe and
   Triumph
Peg Dictionary
Feature Needle
Black Crab
Junior Root
Western Ketchup
Spring Cheetahs
It Princess
Capital Jet
Judas Seahorse
The Often Dropout
Draconian Fun
Leather Purpose
Broke Spate
Party Shiv
The Steam Instant
Fish Kilt
Fur Slur

Squirt Burr
Bed Nails
Curt Husband
Ark of the Motherboard
Kite Pit
Failure Church
Bell Let On
Clean Eaglet
Mummy Corn
Fair Bedtime
Opera Chopper
O. J. Sampson
Grass Bag
Middle Fish
Kitchen Gem
Glaze Rake
Burn Nursery
Jag Gadfly
Bad Cheddar
Gas Leg Iron
Shrink Gin
Larva Card
Sink Beans
Deserve Puree
Clock Pauper
Earn Purge
Pole Solstice
Fat Vacuous
Bend Toward Hamlet
Um Bella

Pail of Chain Mail
Dumb Unicorn
3,000 Coats
Dredging Loch Ness
Asian Mustache
Shimmy Potent
A Classic as Such
Knights in Satan's Service
The Role of More
Red Furniture
Perk Verb
Shaky Handler
The Rose Known as Potion
Jackson Crane
The Bird Worker
Craze Mud
Dab Slash Dab
Crest Pristine
Source Earlier
Fail Sax
Gent Tumbler
Shuffler Cut
Hunt Gleam
Sappy Him
Douse Brand
Beaver Life
Clank Raincoat
Tex Never
Bolter Slaw
The Niggle Given

Fest Estuary
Chip Hippo
Clean Indigo
Houdini Poe
Weekday Crime
Craig Sweater
O. Boaster
Time Slighter
The Entire Rhino
Learning Purr
Single Feast
The Surgeon Version
Special Management Cell
Kicked in the Chest
Barber Shop Laughter
Nitro Tongue
Spent Money Always
Prince Fumer
Turtle Gores
Routine Routine
Different Pang
Persistent Ism
Jumps Off
Rib Kicks
The Frozen Average
The Whole Drop of Water
Fracture Summer
db
Guard God
The Best Doorbells

Idea Magi
Prune Balloon
The Sentence End
Fresh Periscopes
Growler Gaud
So Far Virginal
Prison Handshake
Taffeta Pal
King Made of Weakness
Sty Highness
Dance Fingers
Fedora Orphans
Candy Dress
Past Sashes
The From Plum
Corn Torch
Advantage Sled
Slipper Glass
Midnight in Fairy Tales
Herr True Mettle
Gold Locust
Brick Slippers
Inner Vine
Grand Throat
Mango Clapboard
The Oy Snap
Skilled Ilk
Shore Dolt
Sowing Bugs
Eye Bee

Stupor Student
Steamed Hams
Deadbeat Cheese
Yokel Okay
Buzz Onto
Subject Fun
Must Tomfoolery
Weird Pause
Riding Through Thunder
The Fourth Gradian
Milk Heron
Toggler
Beggar Kettle
Gun Clown
Policy Nozzle
Camper Hammer
Pre Weep
The Leapt Help
Quail Scene
Famous Petticoats
Level Better
Black Ticket Stub
Ice Whites
The And
Laugh a Lot
Wind Dijon
The Line Around Block
Repo Oyster
Regular Headache
Dreaded Wreck

The Food Made
Trinket Buzz
Yesteryear Dredger
Computer Crowbar
Assert Thirsty
Yell Pellet
The Price of a Lifetime
Dank After
Juice Baker
Fed Shortbread
Brawn Comet
Ghoul Pool
The Jaunt Forward
Incredible Pets
Pike Eyebrow
Test Piece
Boondoggle Pose
Fantasy Ape
Detention Fiend
Martini Outcrop
The Clean Demean
The Queen's Family
Sir Charge
Rich Chowder
Late Tootsie
Overall Five
Been Hill
Potty Mao
Dollar Smokes
Bald Pattern

If Thief If
Caste Rat
Rump Clumsy
Best Confession
Small Petty Man
Sour Bank
Ipso Calypso
The Dining Vice
Wet Mile
The Great Wall of
    Childhood
Boat Tail
Next Pest
Hard Pardon
Ike Trifle
Todd Lobsters
The Demonic Possession
    Films
Flirt Reverb
The Noses of the Dead
Putter Croblem
Add Or
Juke Boxful
Sober Flotilla
Goodie Hawthorne
Even River
The Bride Rightly
Beds in Hong Kong
Acne Scab
Hundreds of Cobras

The Role of First Aid
Eerie Meek
Fake Dominate
Smug Turn
Smirk Dummy
Chip Whipper
Penitentiary Tally Marks
The World Donut
742 Evergreen Terrace
Seatbelt Kids
Free Owl
A Sequence of Movements
Alarmist Farm
Damn It Caterpillar
Busted Truck
Space Caves
The Noses of Bid Wisp
Adding Machinist
Cluster Enthusiast
Knot Guilty
Your Cherished Teeth
The True Protectionist
Us Hatcher
Mutton Hole
The Law of Harbinger
Nimble Finish
Correctable Pleasure
Limey Sky
Hector Insert
Magnet Spank

Hot Tub Stunts
Three Mississippi
Bright Pink Bra
Ursula Slush
Gin Christmas
The Fat Proud
Motherloving Flub
The Litigious Kit
Delivery Privy
Mammoth Stomper
Child Scarecrow
Atlanta Sunset
Single Tincture
Pie Fire
The Quick Eye Rub
Whale Fusion
Sugar Supply
Frozen Cornish
Cis Vendor
Clio St. Maria
Workable Head
The Weather Likely
Fung Us
Jeb Syrup
Clout Bronco
Deep Regarder
Vibe Micer
Dagger Slob
Women in Darling Sweaters
Witch Still

A Sequence of Movements

The woman who was also a flower
waved gently as she eased back.
The way her legs unfolded was exactly
as a woman's legs unfold or as a flower
petal might open. She was soft and right
like an idea that grows and grows
till the world begins to incorporate
it into a language, creating vast paragraphs
and the long lashes of winking eyes.
It wasn't true that this woman owned
the world, but it was true that
my own vocabulary was changing.
As the trees climbed high into the air,
as the air was converted by the tree,
so we grew into ourselves, loading
our tired brains with a sort of pudding
that gelled, settling in creases. She
was of a real wave now, swelling
across the surface of the earth. It was
a sequence of movements, like the
steps between a parent and a child.

Best Suited

A thing is lost and yet another
thing is found. Once found, what's
lost gets small in the back of a throat.
Also, birds. Swooping or otherwise
outlining the clouds with invisible
circles. Birds rushing through the
sky. Tall men and moderately sized
women are both found and lost
in a crowd, one at a time, the way
coins are pushed into a parking meter.
A parking spot is lost, another spot
is found. Someone buys loose-fitting
clothing, while another buys clothing
that fits snugger. In some cases, clothes
can be so tight that puzzles assemble
themselves. Still, nothing is seen
that is not unseen. Where there are
mysteries there are solutions. When
there is no time there is time.

Data Choir
Best Suited
Leather Stitches
Stagger Abbot
Plain Airplane
The Wiccan City Planners
Ceiling Door
The Stack Harder
Veil Dolls
The Future Gales
Blood Thump
The Do Get Cross
Truth Phooey
Wallpaper Plot
Gabby Driver
Ruston Kids
Pill Tank
The Reasonable Sadness
Swat Asp
Warlord Bankroll
The Complete Vinegar
The Paradise Drudge
Wound Jinx
Log Forehead
Firm Cancer
The Believe Ping
Odor Fun
The Sole Bummer
Frickin Sister
Stomach Pug

Movie Star Siblings
The Technical Fancier
Pang Anarchy
Face Carver
Buzz Czar
Adept Puncher
Quality Fabric
Issue Free
Whelm Elder
Tanks of Iraq
Fervor Umbrella
Render Spinach
Gnash Bitter
Spun Cuba
Mall Ezra
Un Blunt
Leadbelly Sweater
Elk Sellout
Welcome Muffins
Dry Pike
Constant Bella
Shy Nip
Blight Thou
Agree Feat
Paw Robber
Evidence Locker
Ransom Check
The Failure Ham
The Dressed Midas
Applause Audit

The Echo Stairwell
Theory Bro
Bear Dairy
Bean Allergy
The Improv Swab
The Believe Premise
Pest Inspectors
Goose Shopper
Cookie Tree
Blabber Crab
The Less Ironic Sister
Super Long Fringe
Dread Headroom
Clubfoot Boater
Bong Choices
Sud Nurses
Work Harp
Relax Nabber
Pop Ado
ESP Kisses
Brother's Weeper
The Kill Grits
Butter Pharaoh
Twig Chin
Airplanes in the 1970s
Great Gate
Grace Boy
The Assassin Out
Hunt Hungry
The Quicksand And

The Prominent Fork
Sleepy Bad Guys
Cadet Somewhat
Spike Violence
Genius Spider
Thorn Boner
The Company Chestnut
Flesh Wig
Hand Breaker
Cum Gourmet
Best Fad Ever
Emergency Lips
Goober Hue
Your High School Haircut
Glass Bonus
The Abortion Dole
Together Walkers
Beautiful Sundress
Cheap Pairs
Nose Strudel
Busboy Ties
The Suitor Downtown
Noteworthy Mints
Rust Cup
Dub Trumpet
Slim Toast
Corpse Rum
Bail Maker
The Delicious Chicken
Goal Loader

Four-Hour Erections
Her Ponytail
The Mobile Blood
Knight Ivy
Movie Tragic
First Day Beat Down
Crumb Once
Biker Fight
Forged Orson
Caw Mule
Drape Mailer
Feather Egg
Curl Donor
Glib Ton
Happy Ladder
Salt Robot
Master Chute
Middle Malt
Knee Pain
Beak Tweed
No Mono No
Warning Socks
Slow Burg
Estrada Shield
Medicine Helm
Baby Kidder
Python Gumption
Thrill Litter
Bunk Basement
The Grassy Mole

Bakery Safe
Serial Chill
Deer Penis
Organic Pantsuit
Groan Tumor
The Dark Half Ass
Dead Pimp
Geek Keg
Mutt Seagull
Boon Cougar
Slice Visa
Off-White Stache
Deep Kin
Untrue Meerkat
Spent Money
The Industry Handprints
Gabe Havana
Rock Cast
A Pretty Long List
Fetal Bin
Street Line
Chopped Live
Burn Open
Delay Mush
Ago Alcove
Fire Black
Death Awhile
Womber
The Dead Champ
Alabaster Cab

Kip Lip Prints
Slash Gravitas
No New Hotels
Thud Develop
Each Streamer
Middle School Prayers
Fourth Chair
Rogue Perchance
Peril Particulars
Back Tad
Crimes of Math
Derby Blood
The Obvious Pact
Pill Gunny
Coarse Blade
Ring of Demigods
Hell Pile
Merchant Ape
Play Raise
Miami Beads
Daiquiri Jar
Pill Kilimanjaro
Mt. Fog
Herod's Worst
Bug Grizzle
Swell Velcro
Boom Fox
Cassette Vest
London Chump
Factually Odd

Dorm Mortgage
Mattress Fire
Puffy Robe
Vinegar Skin
Stretch Rhino
Jazz Space Pack
Snore Go-Cart
Interstate Lava
Honey Boot
Tree Sap
Mexico Heaven
Wire Tamper
Stung Punks
Likable Pablo
Married to the Fog
The Cufflink Trophy Case
Toll Fruit
The Situation Bard
Symmetry M's
Whirl Cartel
The Bambi Rant
Ampersand Way
Pork Wine
Peg Depth
Rose Grocer
Gay Blind
The Blow Dart Sergeants
Lawn Art
The Strong Reform
Boundless Drugs

Canker Source
The No Spirits
Sin Missionary
A Better Bible
Pigtail Birther
Pope Adventure
Blind Horse
Treasure Guess
The Possible Bloat
Grandest Can't
Gods of Egypt
Kid Pension
Stock Heir
Oxy Chin
The Big-Time Bluff
Death Paste
Give It Tizzy
The Whiskey Thousand
Sample Fanfare
Brick Distant
Mass Gatling
Cudgel Tusk
Node Polo
Little Dutch
Infant Wheel
Beautiful Pistons
Bit Toe
Boring Folks
Casino Magic
Test Let On

Hard Pillow Talk
Key Weed
Screech Piece
Slowdown Romance
Loretta Grow
Schmuck Pug
Glove Roast
Money Needs
Grey Arcade
Palace Asp
Opt Ore
Prop Less
Heat Kilo
Hit Gambler
Torque Roar
Baby Jailer
God Underage
Police Pod
City Fix
Topless Church
Karate Elvis
The Hardly Yawns
Proven Truman
The Subsequent Guesses
Focused Bloke
Excess Clip
Jugular Faucet
Single Pinko
Band Aid Pace
Went Sinning

Dear Bomber
The Edge Pressure
Now Wowzers
Worse Perfection
Bygone Scotch
Bedevil Westward
The More or Less Coalesce
Thrum Burner
Below Germ
The Callus Offshoot
Brain Strangler
Women Named Goodbye
Perfect Breakup
The Court of Public Onions
Pheasant Melt
The Deserved Version
Hair Chest
Down Cooler
Baton Hombre
Her Red
Like Bub
Crass Inset
Skirt Flipper
Drizzle Kit
World Garçon
Strobe Blanket
Cold Dose
The Chosen Door
Lake Ladies
Barbed Raincoat

It Killer
The Bright White Glow
Wiggler Freedom
Chum Huntsman
Fight Deacon
The Dreams of Tigress
Hug Boat
Raw Propaganda
Student Loan Debt
Moran Nana
Aisle of Olives
The Ever Levity
Xs for Eyes
Sunny Palm Sprangs
Eh Pulpit
The Getting Up Days
The Stopper Clown
The Vanquishers
The Hardly Vacillates
Criminal Apnea
Candle Hands
Furtive Pulse
Core Whiskers
The Least Zenith
The Story of Worry
Age Fader
Squirrel Vandal
Shy Tyrant
Scone Pinsky
Soup Basho

Glue Feet
B Minus
The Itchy Dead
All Four Stomachs
Eight Faker
Born Younger
Dork Snorkel
The Hot Bothered
All Red Tape
Deny Sigh
Bug Fry
Am Sampler
Blow Heart
Boom Millstone
Church Stilts
Brute Hula
Tuxedo Luck
Rash Dino
Bull Tutu
French Bigfoot
Book Tumor
Pearl Worm
Decades of Thursday
Newlywed Danger
All Owls
Mink Wing
Big Top Bed
Russian Luggage
Tad Wonky
Motorcycle Note

Stump Dangler
Silk Eagles
Secret Leggings
Out of the Way Places
Map Dice
Kinder Anton
Ant Gods
Tinier and Tinier
The Beloved Spheres
Cobweb Hot Tubs
Careful Anders
The Shovel Betters
The Front Door Gun
Brownie Oinks
Big Shot Goners
Prof Corsage
Newly Ten Foot
The Marriage Square Knot
Celeb Elbow
The Ultimate Felix
Mini Whoop
Twinge Benefit
Tempo Gem
Say It Egg
Balloon Lynch
A Fair Life
Sad No Ones
The Imperfect Reed
Twee Evil
Moot Only

Geez Pillows
Pert Cedric
Soul Leaks
Dollar Fridges
The Orange Staples
Tooth Canoe
Face Haze
Ruby Backseat
Warm Speedos
Butter Socks
Bomb Tease
Paid in Tridents
The Lamp Dids
Bone Link
The After-Awhile Pie
Zoom Cameras
Straw Umps
Doom Mood
Furniture Burn
Record Teapot
Earner Hen
Coward Quack
Safe Vary
Suckish Shoes
Monk Sponges
Mojo Spittle
Beyond Ottawa
Trojan Notebook
Sleeping Beg
Melt Buckles

Ben Up
Nag Lazarus
Scar Depository
Agent Risk
Air Package
Birth Ordinate
The Pain Belief
The Turn Ox
Further Mustard
Outdoor Flesh
The Snake Vogue
Metro Briefcase
Will Spillage
@ U

The Lives of Writers

Bare Igor
Cat Toaster
Me Totem
Full Fax
Drag Haircut
Two Figure Payday
Firefight Win
Closet Search
Additional Stride
Off ER
After Joke
Massive Pulley
The Won Worst
Calf Telepath
Pour Poor

The Lives of Writers

One famous writer says another famous writer
couldn't write his way out of a paper bag
and then some other writer writes, "Well,
so-and-so's writing is like wading
through beef gravy." Another writer says, "Last
time I read her, I threw up a little in my
mouth and had to rush to the bathroom lest
I get vomit-foam on my beard—Really, it's
just the writing—it's so bad." Another writer
says, "I want to like her work but it just
takes so much damn work to read that horrible
prose." A famous or less famous writer might
say the same about a third, semifamous
writer. They say, "That writer just writes
bad sentences. The sentences are so bad."
One writer, who writes reviews, writes of
another writer, "He seems to have never learned
the difference between a good sentence and
a life sentence." "The writing is really, really
terrible," says another writer, chiming in with
the writer earlier. That earlier writer says,
"I too agree with what I said." A writer who lives
in a warm climate might say of a writer
who lives in a less warm climate (though perhaps still
quite humid), "I have chilled to this writer's

writing—it's moist and not any good!"
A writer of great renown says of a former friend,
who is also a writer, "I should have known he'd
be a boring writer by the eulogy
he delivered at that other writer's funeral, whose
death relieved the world of a very constipated writer."
Another writer, this one a little taller than some
other writers, says, "Her writing comes up
short, it fails to attain the proper height."
A writer we previously haven't considered
writes of a writer we will not read about for a long time
to come, "That writer is a bad writer who
can cause your eyes to spin freely in their sockets."
Another writer who was unmentioned before
now says of a writer you actually met once
(by chance—in an airport), "He
is trying to write, bless his putrid little heart."
A writer is older than another writer and says,
"Perhaps, they still have time to learn the difference
between helping a reader or murdering one."
One writer, who frequently uses sexual imagery
says, "That writer makes me want to become a
eunuch, begging him not to violate me with the shit-
sausage that is his sentence construction." It really
goes on and on. Another writer says a
dismissive comment about another writer because,
she says, "The writing just isn't any good. At all."

"It's quite simple," says this one writer, "There is good writing and there is bad writing. How that other writer, the one who writes so badly, became a mystery writer is a mystery to me." There's really no end to one writer saying another writer doesn't know how to write. It goes on and on. A writer who has good taste says, "That writer has horrible taste, my god!" Some writers get really indignant. Some even stay up late, arguing with other writers in long, tense emails.

Careful of the Panther

Careful! The panther over there
has eyes on you and is crouching
in a manner that makes me think
of pouncing and that's no good for you.
That panther is troubled, too. He has
secrets he keeps from himself, erupting
in bloody gore-orgies, involving claws,
teeth and the muscles of the jaw.
Also, that panther has no scruples.
His brain doesn't seem to register
the emotions of others. He's wild.
His coat is dark and oily, but he
wears it not for the lady panthers,
but for the humans. To them he
mouths, "You are a stack of meat."
Also, that panther has biked the dirt
trails of your youth and he'll floss
his teeth with the veins of your neck.

The Rerun Moes
Global Skates
German Surf
The Fifth Deep
Semi Final
Iffy Riff
The Third-Place Trophy
Glib Gripe
Miss Skyward
Meat House
Richer Stevens
Goodnight Broadcaster
Evermore Chain
The Nose Position
Provisional Keepsake
Word Doorway
Finger Gag
The Appropriate Toilets
Tougher Bunnies
Guest Sect
Verbal Slaw
Nadia Riot
Wicked Damp
Def Cousin
The Steep Free
To Owe Amos
Brief String
The Clap Faster
The Stoked Total
The Wait Case

Downward Gown
One Pound Fig
Weird Goals
Hotel Shellfish
Tightwad Wife
Sweaters I Made You
Sauce Bottles
The Swami Salt
The Rainbow Burn
Stand Abash
The Main Ambush
Sock Money
Goose Tush
Cigar Fire
A Smaller Mall
The Lay-Down Craze
Ow Moscow
Guile Hydrant
Born Chemical
Thirst No One
Downtown Airport
Cabinet Presley
Gallstone Bow
Careful of the Panther
Polite Nightly
Firm Go Code
Robber Mullet
The Garden on Down
The Gold Neck Chains
Stolen Limbs

Pro Convoy
Carnival Hog
Lord Dum-Dum
The Car Rolling Over
Fourfold Flood
Philly Food
Yarn Some
Bark Barn
Nose Pleas
The Bargain Because
Leap Dozer
Double Mud
Fireworks or the Storm
You Being You
Book Blower
Nine Central
Cereal Palsy
Jeweler Feed
Story Jorge
Seven Almonds
First Kid
Anaheim Bank Job
Hint Mannequin
Special Headwear
Tedious Wig
Win Owner
Come Die
Sting Fingerly
Hungry Young
The Program Mantra

Lingering Garbage
The Tissue Test
Bunyan Cool
The Posted Results
Prima Comma
Sober Friday
Spy Eyelet
Twin Him
Trigger Napkins
Triumph Caveat
Trust Gerbils
The Ebb Crisis
Maple Ape
Note Billions
The Un Glow
Pig Tenure
Sick Treats
Dis Ember
Peanut Guts
Dead Sum
Crib Security
The Spurt Sport
Village Idea
Multi Asker
Wry Price
Water Plant
The Deduct Cubby
The Key Lease
Convention Fibs
Hum Rumble

A Funnier Gotham
Goner Box
Step Pet
Starched Dollar
Drunk Boss
Trucker Goon
Aldo Also
Clay Sail
The You Wouldn't Care
No Javier
Casanova Stars Out
Otis Throat
Scrimshaw Cloud
Pleat Keith
Net Teflon
Abject Yak
Bat Portion
Smooch Workshop
Tinny Dingo
Specialty Meat
Sculpture Berg
Swelter Mutt
Kale Whale
Torture Word
The Rewind Dude
Gay Stepson
Jung Fungus
Spelling Elbow
Neurological Haw
Shame Manchild

Two O'clock Equal
Jerk Bungalow
Monologue Law
Prop Mongoose
Drivel Igloo
Can of Mail
The Dribble Penchant
Fig Sickle
So Asymptomatic
The Skim Micks
Sleet V
Dreg Pedal
Hand Kind
Moose Tula
Grist Eardrum
Cable Mooch
Ginormo Dice
Stay Festus
Viking Life
Swimmer Will
The Is Pester
Cork Diet
Polite Body
Globe Pony
Need Eater
Ere Develop
Win Neither
Char Arp
Lots of Endings
Scorpio Light Rod

Check Pleasure
Nothing But Opinions
Pillbox Slugger
Acci Dent
Bye Killer
Real Down Taxi
Double Eager
Saxophone Space
Girl Hornet
Unpainted Ain't
Suddenly There Is Change
Soup Pink
Troop Fir
The Greenest of Green
The Blown Aslant
Packaged Me Too
The Very Very Suspicious
The Hip Observant
Moses Trench
Screw Head Is
Gasp Tabernacle
Warm Yogurt
School Radios
The Styrofoam Flat Hats
Center Paw
Rose Crowbar
Walnut Creepers
Swindle Ham
The Garnish Overly
Quip Wood

Iris Liner
Drugs for Everyone
Minor Nor
One Hip
The Ginger Least
Narc Honest
The Sand Beneath Our Feet
Going Away Hey
Black Saccharine
The Della Lungs
The Freewheel Nowhere
Florid Order
Cave Mane
The Equipment Jukes
Fanfare Higher
Short Hoister
Crepe Paperweight
The Detailed Bible
Safe Lamp
Treasure Owl
Game Mother
Farm Flood
Core Peaches
Drunk Ribbon
Nose Fire
Frail Letter
The Blue Glove Ocean
Important Death Scenes
Neck Buddy
Parka Car

Nest Keg
Dang I.V.
The Hinge Gimme
Section Things
Bend O Bend
The First Aubrey
Seven Whimpers
The Fish You Catch
King Deer Head
Fuzz Shrink
Silly Pie
People Amnesia
The Getting Dinners
The Coed Drop Dead
Amp Dancer
Ghost Figurines
Civil Bendover
Chick Fidget
Devilled Legs
Super White Pie
Disco Isn't
Barstool Pants
A Might Nervous
Energy Whip
Heck Guess
The Stupor Grew
Stateless Hospital
The Laundry Moving
Horn Rim
Doyle Boy

Light Funny
The Recollect Etch
My Dead Daddy
The Rooster Book
The Socket Gets
Quiet Spelling
The Tolerable Huff
Cough License
The Begot Logic
Hump Loud
The Gone Balder
Family Hank
Dealt Fan
Monster Site
Terrible Gentle
Each & Every Deadbeat
Me & the Tan Equipment
Jaw Dogged
Now Slow
Vaughn Orchid
The Key People
The Employee Discounts
Boiled Milk
Kid Hitman
Landmine Righto
Fatter Knot
Really Lily
Danger Fink
Hell Level
The Apology Set

Dual Buttons
The Shop Proper
Stuck Burrs
The Figure Reel
Voice Pork
The Probably Arc
The Good Rules
Stone Thanks
Biscuit Moon
The Recent Back
Shady Waiters
The Clung
Stereo Hands
The Yonder Off
The Manacle Or
Early Stump
Might Meaner
Slang Aim
The Arm Around
Young Gunk
The Lawn Nowadays
The Hard Starve
The Cord Plug
The Mess Up North
Mouth Tape
The Friend Hints
The Warehouse Blues
The Struggle Underfoot
Nothing Seemed Right
The Drink from Nowhere

The Under Sand
Trumpet Runts
In Guise
Harpo Marge
The Pouring Sweater
Fact Tango
Sprinkler Goop
The Pizza Isn't
Yarn Curtain
Famous Stammer
Perfectly Girlfriend
Nose Redwood
Soda Monk
Got Dot
Lest Fingers
Nellie Pleasant
Can't Can't Can't
Plastic Ashtrays
Prior Rib
Fanny Plan
The Rosie Obligation
Maw Waistcoat
Team Meat
Brink Greaser
Fairly Derelict
Pet Stretcher
The Didn't Loophole
Glare Err
The Get Fancy
Cat Ladle

Nothing Seemed Right

"There's no way to unwire the spring lever
once you've pushed that little plastic piece
out of the threaded area," is what I was saying
when it became obvious I should focus
on something else. The motor? No. The Claw?
No. Nothing seemed right. I tilted my head
and adjusted the collar buckled to the arm.
Marching in the distance, whole branches
of the military. I was lonely because everything
in life leads to loneliness but I held onto
to hope because it was invisible and I could
pretend it was everywhere. A little thought
was creeping in my mind on insect legs,
beginning to infect my vision.

The Positions around the Extractor

The extractor was a set of jaws with a series
of pulleys and misunderstandings that caused
feeble people to weaken their knee bones
and cast hardened shadows at the floor.
One particular vacuum incubator, Tim, a sort
of drizzly fellow with a serpentine disposition,
found a hole in the equipment organizer
and so pulverized the back cork that there was
never a rumble from the kitchen within. Rose,
the woman behind the land rush, made every
situation even more squat and brackish. Also,
Jim, the magician of uprising, became grossly
indifferent to the shag-skin tears and the veiled
threats coming from Ms. Worthington.
"Alas," said Ms. Worthington, "my swollen gut
will no longer fashion an extractor regulator
from the Wise-Apple Glee Corporation." "In fact,"
said Sister Ripple of Cutting Coarse, "Every ounce
of silver will wrap around this vacancy until pretty
much all salted happiness has a chance of
swooning." "O wobbly wheel," cried the orphan,
Scott. The orphan Scott was alone in the crib
he would never climb out of because he was
dead and no extractor could change that.

Trial Firefly
Net Red
The Tourney Resort
Nervous Service
Your Jury
Bad Struggler
Caper Pay
Perv Nuggets
Bedpost Rope
Darling Gas Tank
Kids and Video Games
Boot Muse
Abraham Charm & the
    Neck Beards
Flower Toss
Factory Atrophy
Sap Abbot
Mullah Fuel
Oozero
Eternal Oil
Crude Vladimir
Pressing Importance
Bred Hello
The Is It
Stern Foreleg
The Week of July
Leaf Raker
Tush Bushel
Dip Outright
The Jumps Sometimes

Turn Clutch
Foil Skirt
The French Accomplice
Slight Carrot
The Coffin Offer
Load Pause
The Real Quitting
Rad Braid
The Hideous Tilt
Über Festoon
Mule Flute
Group Tool
Red Thread
Lush Fund
The Young Number
The Only Zone
Swan Mogul
Phew Phooey
Due Dew
The Was Saw
Back Fat
The Positions around the
    Extractor
Pink Ankles
School Foot
Oswald Sauté
Bullet Pup
Outlaw Bricks
Pow Typhoon
The Sketch Welcome

Bunk Comb
Skull User
The V in Even
Concert Effigy
Lou Cruel
Dingbat Gnats
Skimpy Reason
Vegan Thor
The Easy Crease
The Glut Lucky
Knife Rise
Win Gloss
Shake Pleaser
Net Bunker
Station Vey
Ordinary Hair
Goodbye Plato
Spruce Noose
Tepid Pit
Farm Star
Fist Dig
Case of Cobwebs
Honor Rat
Pronto Lounge
Outer Heart
Gut Tug
Text Cray
Emory Bender
Child Spite
The Green Green Greens

Miles of Why
Mass Herder
The Trash in Big Cities
Glib Tricks
Bather Face
Iron Rung
Sea Pea
The Go At
Happy Pass
Close Handler
Narrow Party
The Bomb Squid
The Jitter Minimum
The Eleven Set
Kid Snivel
The Previous October
Fed Decade
End Mint
The Seem Meeker
The Proper Tall
Flag Boss
Deviant Knees
Rug Custody
Cope Funder
Cleft Lung
Wax Target
The Fledgling Edge
Baby Grate
Apple Stuff
Plunge Proof

The True Neuter
Pot Heart
Dance Fang
Nar Nuzzle
A Sniper Scene
Dunk Judas
Pylon Eye
The Right Fig
12 Stepbrothers
Hidden Soup
The History Give Up
The Full Mule
The Slow What
Violin Plums
Someone Bombing Dresden
Smote Goat
Lenin and Trotsky Arguing
Kip Pillar
Banned Bye-Bye
Gumbo Tent
Only Phones
One Whole Lude
Cabbage Festival
Senior Pancake
Leather Cherry
Soul Jealous
Best Yoko Ever
Dry Lick
Gored Ham
Burly Urge

Fudge Dump
Dally North
Bypass Chest
Muddy French
Pub Guppy
Yak Cast
Vow Down
Insta Instance
Free Punch
Six Hundred & Sixty-Six
Airport Blood
Compound Stomp
Eve Sleeve
Liable Science
Nine Blanks
Pinprick Hemorrhages
Cyber Fire
Nose Mud
Slab Tabby
Your Wren
Ex Axe
The Song Tongs
Joan No Eyes
The Rightly Smiles
Hip Pituitary
Ripe Corker
Top Off
Light Pie
Stuffed Taker
Money Boo

Tug Fishes
Movie Scars
Rife Tightly
Crawl Talons
Paw Paw Paw
Big Fox
Dreg Heavens
Corner Messes
Spider Diet
Rat Hack
Thinking About Fire
World's Largest Family
Great Bassist
Deacon Light Source
Pixel Sick
Glitch Pistol
Fragment Pa
Tattle Gnat
Ponzi Sympathizer
The Wait Lose
Just Deserts
Beat Swans
Trigger Yawning
The She Carnage
Wig Zag
Drag Pie
Mince Swift
The Whole Doldrums
Behoover
Glam Pandora

Polly Feral
Bling Gifter
The Not Leon
The Into Hints
Purse Work
The Airplane Substantial
The Personal Think Beyond
Furious Hirsute
Over Toads
The Kremlin Snow Ghosts
Burn Science and the
    So Addled
The Crane Technique
Rosewood Pins
The Go Suddens
The My Vibe
The Totally One Thing
Land Sicko
The Politeness
A Brief How
The Eyebrow Stage
Rue True
Pie High Top
Lick Minded
Daisy Ruin
Coal Lotus
The Bright Light of Bee
    Season
Microwave Rum
Style Perchance

Roast Loco
Thick Price
Sir Adrian
Lax Lust
The Far Bind
The Story Bored
Wind Perp
Ouch Org
State Heathens
Predict Typo
My Latest Issue
Wrecker Said So
Half Tad
Payola Yokel
Stomach Flies
All Tsar Team
Jerk Perk
Stale Ram
Cummer Samp
Bust Rub
The Fear Most
Prodigal Dot
Veil Pipe
Used Sugar
Pear Rarity
The Theist Fees
All Over Antlers
Buzz Lawyer
Yep Coop
Chew Portals

Lame Lab Partners
Free Doodlers
Dystopia Me
Eager Jeepers
Promo Committee
Vole Headrest
Juanita Always
Head Gathers
The Disrobe Home
A Quicker Guillotine
Little Deadly
Bit Jealous
Mattress Glass
Pile Nice
The Watch Out Even
Top Sped
The Coolest Kids in
   the World
Fanny Chance
Goner List
Chef Dad
T. S. Oedipus
The Servant Must
Spark Farm
Grass Plaque
Onto Noon
Glacier Lunch
Poison Doily
Slump Organ
Long Biz

The Before Normal
Nag Grandeur
Weed Raincoat
Older Woe
Taking the Banner Down
Lawn Doughnuts
Feisty Behind
Rap Apple
Moon Cooler
Quality Octopus
Boss Soap
Ease Freak
The Diet of Jesse James
Kid Prison
Perestroika Soy
Gander Flange
The Company Eel
Graffiti Feed
Moor Liam
Cedar Mop
Pom-Pom Boys
Bunk Knub
The Supreme Itty
Ernest Purse
Mob Orders
The Grow Weirdly
Grass Throb
Corn Junket
The Going Sash
Helper Donkey

Feeble Heap
Sir Doris Do
Jolly Mags
Charmer Zing
Pews Naper
Phony Pesos
Nana Anna
Breeze Neither
Cover Fruit
Mo Jo
Car Fat
Smoother Than Saturn
Chi Christ
Cog Datcher
Head Thermos
Peg Gets
Admiral Cipher
Hum Puss
War Den
The Civic Bilk
Super Ham
Regal Lager
Don Nod
Bell Y'all
Air Goats
The Chance Organic
Pout Toupee
The Wrong Faster
A Might Higher
Cheek Streets

The Diet of Jesse James

O, Jesse James ate cash, mostly, but he
also ate other forms of money, like
checks and bank statements. He drank
water, whiskey and his own vomit.
He once enjoyed his mom's country
cooking and ate mouse pie, gravy
and an interesting variety of potato.
He also once carried a gun and robbed
banks, but this only concerns his diet
in a tangential way. He was good on
a horse, but this, sadly, doesn't matter in
regard to his diet. His brother, too, is also
not a matter that concerns his diet. No,
his diet was mostly cash and other forms
of money, most of which he never paid
for. O, his diet raises very uncomfortable,
but necessary, questions. No, they are not
easy to answer but they must be asked
when considering the diet of Jesse James.

Changing Directions

"Let's change directions," said the captain.
"Yes, let's go this way," said the chaplain.
"Let's have a go at North," said the first mate.
"And a go at South," added the captain.
"And a go at South, indeed," said the first mate.
"So we agree?" said the first mate.
"We certainly do," said the second mate.
"And the third mate?" asked the chaplain.
"On board," responded the second mate.
"Indeed," said the third mate, "On Board."
"That's delightful," said the captain.
"Let's change directions again," said the captain.
"Yes, let's go another way," said the fourth mate.
"Yes, another direction," echoed the captain.
"Yes, another direction," reechoed the chaplain.
"Chaplain," said the captain, "Does God feel in one direction or another in terms of the direction we go?"
"Not at all," says the chaplain, "God feels directions change and begrudges no direction."
"Well, then let's change directions," said the cook.
"I agree with the cook," said the first mate.
"I agree with the cook as well," said the second mate.
"Yes, the cook," said the captain, "The cook, indeed."

Mercy Ghee
Garden Hardtop
Stash Pony
The Nut Tons
Changing Directions
All Partly
Old Sherbet
Peal Leastwise
Blanket Hey
The Synth In
Sink Fins
Harbor Dolls
Machete Fed
Real Live Heartaches
What Reagan Didn't Do
Less Pegasus
Theory Crank
The Doling Opera
Finch Surrender
The Igloo Stupid
Monde Blom
Harm Détente
The Je Ne Sais Quoi Otter
Flyaway Goodnights
Pet Detester
The Gift of Dead Languages
The Better Part of a
    Half Hour
Hi Graves
Shin Pinch

A Future Beginning with
    Orphans
Stomp Ethos
Liar White
The Kidder Dick
Plight of Firewood
Safe Wraith
The Give None Poe
Pope Escort
Hut Tulips
The Never Mind Rats
Clean Pangs
The Eight Ohs
The Favorite Aprons
Hit Depot
Slim Fib
The Shirts Beneath Their
    Coats
Sleep Peels
The Lew Do
Super Great Farmhands
Orca Perm
Sorta Rapture
Claw Walk
The Enterprising All
    the Way
The Bonus Prone
Leather Curb
The Notebook Next to
    Nothing

Finger Easter
The Dry Ice Stagecraft
The First Cordless Phones
The Store Whacko
The Pipes Really
Stage Four Bagpipe
Tight Hydrants
The Perfectly Timed
    Mighty
The Drink Fitful
Famous Pagans
Clear Merv
Numb Ergo
Bed Yarn
Mini Uni
Almond Lung
The Vegetable Rows
Blood Frosting
Cheese Beak
The Cure for Cancun
Cater Paces
The Is Cricket
Boa Noise
The Crochet Vote
Iron Eye
The Fell All Over
    Themselves
Perm Loudmouth
Swiss Neutral
The Ester Nest

Fun Muscle
The Tank Left
Jeez Thieves
Though Porous
Love Ruckus
The Costlier
The Dim Mid
Skeet Pita
Bogus Lancer
Flub Pastors
Speaker of the Blouse
Gentle Clinker
Housedog Nobility
Lemonade Fist
Usually Ether
Axe Shower
Anyhoo Gay
Citywide Tamper
Rapt Breakdown
Custom Gusto
Soot Hootenanny
Scatter as Good
Mad Wow
The Value Pang
Certain Hot Valves
Fluffier Hurt
The Cute Noodles
Officer Way Up
The Peel Kneel Down
Retro Pose

Loss Dossier
Trust Hustler
My Pal Avarice
Cheat Piqué
Cull Onward
Stone Quotient
Smitten Bigger
Piglet Signet
Lil Neither
Alimony California
The Chore Snorkels
Slather Package
Robe Bellicose
Dead Pleasant
The Beelzebub Elite
Her Bodice Apart
The Tolerable Lifelong
Pretty Headroom
The Ought to Resolve
Hitherto Rueful
Gibbet Ending
Futile Meekly
Computer Beg
The Said Regulator
The Elapsed Nod
Staid Pyro
The Visible Istanbul
Grief Reef
Noontide Sublime
Granite Fib

The Stars Up for an Award
The Vice Presidential Picks
Advantage Tanner
Purr Urchins
Tyrannosaurs Next
Card Guards
Jonestown Orange
Least Reaper
Till Bit
Guano Fawn
Callus Trust
Granola Soul
God Module
The Pivot Ing
The Triumphant Fro
Rockcoach
Bee R
Brisk Igor
Chic Shtick
Epic Enters
Really Quite Convenient
Flour Boar
Gee Orator
The Larger Cement Truck
Roman Flitting
Thudder Butt
Howler Bat
Ball Parts
Little Comfort
Blood Luddite

Her Capita
Mocker Chaos
The Transition Taking Place
The Circuitry Terms
The Formidable Brian
Neural Nets
Post Fight Hairdo
Virtual Slipstick
Blind Clinton
Dry Algorithm
Representing a Problem
Essentially Zero
Only the Correct Solution
Brown Velvet Bean
The Accost Often
Swept Up in It
Bomb Office
Gauze Headbands
The Broom Made of Revelations
Ply Ossify
Sheen Renter
The Message Loon
What We Know of Life
The Etta Set
Huger Took
Plaid Clad and Versify
The Tint Unorthodox
Co Defendants
Hunker Bifocals
Soft Attractor
Types of Straw Hats
Timothy Moth
Theta Cesspool
The E Machine Readout
World Tin Wrist
The Geography of No Place
The Slower Kilo
The Way to Address the Tenth Row
The Clear-Cut Acne
Palace Lab
The Conspired to Steal
Outsider Recess
Bang Sidearms
Cusp Justice
The Vetting Cleans
The Mincing Into
Dust Eater
Dig Gist
Sycophant Caucus
Newt Ring
Twin Nips
Hush Invaded
Suture Intruder
Umpteen Newbies
Stale Ebola
Smear Marta
The Preserve and Fanfares

Thy Yolo
Chap Tribe
Thrice Thine
Scurry Rup
Owed Toenails
Confessing to Murder
Poor Adultery
Three Pool Useless
The Give Petro Please
Letting in the Dog
The Politicians in
    Washington
Winter Pillow
Scatman Furtherz
Wings Gone Salty
The Rising Cost of
    Entertainment
Milk Skimmer
Tore-Up Gut
Wolf Kitchen
Buena Vista Free
Kelp Ellington
Stereotypical Villains
Nine Out of Ten
Fun Chaperon
Teen Malcontents
Paris Gophers
Pudding Tube
And Comeuppance
Lie Ideation

Deadly Pastry
The Impotent I Am
Wow Dowel
Tack Baxes
Dead Segregation
Mutt Mud
Lousy Pie
Zeus Food
Heedless of Ithaca
Trojan Horse Guts
Overcoat Bromide
The Invention of
    Silhouettes
Electro Fork
Joan of Anarchy
The Conquer Dauphin
The Arrow Wars
Bucket Fire
Thinner Center
Classic Asteroid
Mo Hope
Melt Sweater
Bird Usurper
Poison Ear
Damn Hamlet
Fear of Stabbing
Revenge Prince
Paw Meat
Blown Gages
Swarm Hundred

Devoid Coy	Coal Locust
Ceramic Rib	Cope Polo
Chez Psychiatric	Vice Eyebrows
Belly Heat	Hog Golly
The Frequent Quills	Roger Cutoff
Clinical Roofer	Cloven Roofers
Twirling Alfredo	Snake Dresser
50 Percent Awesome	Deny Deny Deny
The Science Blab	Dollar Knots
The Mundane Lumps	Stomach Haste
Spacesuit Rudolph	Number Hunkers
Beauty Huge	Kyle Crisis
The Rooster	Tuition Shoe
Fangs a Lot	Tongue Dummy
The So What Bloat	Bear Rarity
Late Model Pedal	The Subject Foot Rub
The Attacker ID	Awhile Likely
The Bankruptcy Solo	Whistler Prism
The Coin Flips	Filigree Significant
Prison Lip Print	The Parole Ordeal
Black Reno	The Fair Merit
Together Questions	Score Portal
Prison Pending	Proto Moto
The Institution End	Ghetto Yellow
Lineup Ideals	Altogether Messy
The Early Infer	The Expired Little Guy
Rum Muscle	Bug Nixon
The Profane Frontal	The Abject Duplex
Wrinkle Free Dome	Gel Sweatshop
Apropos Go	The Reparation Freight

The Rooster

We couldn't correct the rooster
because the rooster would not
humble himself to the authority
of the court, much less us. His beak
high in the fashion of a prince, his
eyes with a light like a candle
by a bed in the dark. More than
once I personally rebuked him,
publicly and privately, with the
hope of restoring order and sense,
with the swollen intention
of causing happiness for the vast
many of us, wading in the mess
he was making. Even the duchess
of shadowy milk tried to pour
some sleek redemption over
the hard apple of his bitterness.
But the rooster would not budge.
The rooster, ignoring everyone,
befriended the local musicians
and started a band. The rooster
toured the East and West Coasts,
making the most of his feathered
wings, squawking and clawing the
crowds about their temples. Leaving

marks an inch deep in the cheeks
of his audience. Making sure, being
positive, that we would bow to his
rooster power, that we would lay
down our lives so that he might live.

Sure Icky
Imagination Plato
The White Cliffs of Europe
Nuck Chorris
The Small Roll Off
The Given Bed Clothes
Agnew Crooks
Watergate Clumps
The Fake Blind
The Devil Via Talk Show
The Leave Peek-a-Boo
The Late Said
Heavy Bread Bowl
The Dream Vicious
Butter Night
Tech Weeper
Oil Liar
The Jar Finger
Fad Matter
The Lowly Dinner Roll
Secret Nickels
Fight Slice
The Drive Through
    the Valley
Friend Equipment
Team A and Team B
Tall Gawk
Furlough Notebook
Bio Eyelid
Roll Smokes

The Just Found Out
Seven Years
Ned of Bails
Men in Temperate Jackets
The Short Dollar Say-So
Jut Function
Raining Squid
Over William Told
Cloth Sign
Joy Such
A Regal Orange
Deep Treaty
Attaché Face
Helmet Elf
The Is Auspicious
Aviator Brace
The Don't Go In
Stepping on Stepstools
Glee Amigo
Chake Snarmer
The Venom Limp
Barber Arson
The Current Zeke
Carpet Sharks
The Sooner Tomb
Baby General
The I Am Pamphlet
Shamb
Pony Boner
Body Fires

Cork Roman
Ass of All Trades
Moses Peacoat
Best Vulgate
Hanging Traders
Hick Boil
The Occult Hoard
Bygone Slinky
Pudgy God
Dick Wind
Plague Ruler
Pip Notion
Ghost Shank
Before the Sun Goes Down
See Framples
Half-Pipe Pharisees
Amen Hamper
Rah Rah Farrah
Easy Earth
Pecan Poets
Star Carpool
Working for Free
Tedious and Unpleasant
Yeast Money
Cake File
Fashionable Daughters
Adult Onsetter
Cookie Soot
Milk Bright
Quart of Origami

Car Rot Orange
A Position of Comfort
Bro Thunder
Diagnosis Pyro
Stolen Crutches
Summer Salad
Day Cape
The Contagious Stub
Can Deacons
Hospital Sugar
Flarf Workshop
Eyelid Peelers
The Best Kept Cretins
The Manifest Knot
The Beautiful Parade Did
Art Smart
The Role of Parasites
The Real Life Ending
Canary Bear
Shit Repartee
The Somewhat Among Us
The Food Um
The Can't Sanctuary
Lava Snap
The Fold Under
The Needle Severe
The Question of Raincoats
Velocity Lot
Prussian Uppers
Animal Fan Belt

Rubber Fort
The Set Few
The Keep Listless
The Were Perfect
Tide Diaper
Raul Mess
Host Elegy
Tube of Miracles
Useful You
Zoo Ooze
Feline Rind
Regular Leper
Horse Bone
Morning Gulag
Verbaler
Bay Clay
Warning Punk
Scorn Coping
Swamp Pups
The Blah Haphazards
Loot Focker
Bull Mechanic
Nuzzy Favel
Happily Ever Before
Ant Uncle
Plunging into Mirrors
Brass Knuckle Babies
Mule Dude
City Zen
Lousy Grouser

More or Less Certain
Airtight Syllabi
Burly Circus
Proper Head Case
O Hobo
The Extent of Pidgins
Chum Much
Battlefield Pianos
Buzzard Mud
Song Donkey
Boy Zing
Fig Drizzler
Sty Cyclops
Tender Limbs
Drawl Hauler
The Tap Aptly
Bat Calf
Custard Mutt
The Growing Up and
   Growing Old
Yep Mongoose
Nerd Yearns
Iffing Gift
Narcolepsy Heart
Bar Pharmacy
Beulah Fruit
Sass Fairly
The Alpha Bled
Stun Nuts
Fixed Meelings

Chemo Chin
Mob Toppler
Gloom Poodle
The Very Scenario
Loving Marsha Brady
Moon Tune-Up
Splice Iron
Free Cheek
Somber Bombay
Pucky Lenny
Pinch Fault
Guest Bread
Celebration Fade
Your Stepkid Best
The Growth Mostly
Rip Leader
Sour Towel
Fargo Supermarket
The Digestive Humor
All Sharks in the Ocean
Tall Cat Lady
Cheer Sidney
Liablizer
Crater Aprons
Rid Leaper
The Nourish as Such
Claim Boliviano
Ennui Juniper
Starlight Pie
Hume Loosely

Born Adorno
Three Bright Nicely
Patch Advocates
Yes Satan
The Runt Crunch
Given Bikini
Barge Throaty
Gland Pandora
Angelo Foot Rub
Hush Mug Shot
Gravy Sweater
Blush Suckle
Now Wadding
Language Apes
The Fab Backdrop
Runny Pose
Fungus Altos
The Ocean Goes Whish
Foot Veins
Delano Pod
Bro Mauler
The Tries Pica
The Benefit of the Pout
Swig Litany
Pole Faults
Chill Vindictive
Bulldog Gods
The Orange Candidates
Bunny Stop
Kilo of Downers

The Verily Pitchforks	The Suffer Fuss
Jinx Kin	The Poly Obsoletes
Beige Tail	Sog Noggin
Quality Art War	The Vacillate Savior
Dig Jo Jo Dig	Tender Them
Defeatist Hourglass	Scarce Heirs
The Commercial Returns	Bail Fetters
The Vague Band Name	Looter Food
Slower Puma	The Electron And
Aero Dynamite	Ego Ado
Pity Finals	Out Limes
Glow Overage	Beeline Needs
Accomplish Mink	Prog Frog
The Poets of Ghana	Enough Butler
Fun Wok	The Way She Lets Go
Winsome Tidbits	The Same Ambulance
Mistook Hoopla	The Icky Gizmos
The Deflect Lecture	Wormhole Aces
Bootstrap Fashion	Black Daiquiri
Country Eggs	Plain Santos
Humble Understanding	Brick Underling
The Loyal Sock Gag	Sir Real Privy
Head Touched	The Savor Pace
Value Adder	Govern Rug
Her Clear Exceptions	Font Brothel
Conviction History	Mint Girdles
Account Rightly	Nasty Staffer
Applied Apples	Tizzy Imps
Odd Coddler	The Afford Sword
The Pled Deadly	Juice Rooster

Fun Clip
Twinge Members
The None Fund
Scotch Ratchet
Slang Angler
Security Inch
Swing Boater
Ernest Thang
Too Many Politicians
Piecemeal Weakling
The As Patter
The Natural Fast
Easy Sendoff
Snag Hatch
Tweed Abuse
Speaker Needs
The Exceptional Cursive
Cue Igor
Senator Freak
Germ Fervor
Elicit Pickle
Oboe Nose
Go Mosquito
Can't Andy
Glue Nun
The Sole Rub
Hun Grumble
Lank Dough
Sauna Anna
Yawn Hottie

Aroma Chrome
Given Toledo
Barn Farmers
Silo Boos
Wedge Tissue
Beep Tray
Cluff Baller
Glamour Shat
Greed Feaster
Emergency Quakers
Short Snort
Lil Stitch
The Diction Wary
Ass Jawbone
Pea Hive
The Chest Sores
The Beloved Museum
Gonad Nadir
Gasp Havoc
DJ Tanner Rant
Lake Cadence
Pup Strings
Bad Sass
Growler Ow
Prig Fit
What Matters
Chuck Annul
The Way Disco
The Agenda Swimmer
Jaundice Blonde

What Matters

The man was singing to the children
but the children weren't listening
"Because," they said, "we are wearing
wet blankets and beyond the ability
to matter." "What's that about matter?"
said the man. "About what?" said one
child who was as pink as a balloon.
"I'm worried about the antimatter," said
the man, "I admit it might be foolish
but the antimatter troubles me deeply.
Similar to a map that is marked up
by a visiting General. He's drawing arrows
here and drawing arrows there and
lining up battalions and whatnot,
but deep down, in the geography of the
moment, a sense of antimatter is
running down the backs of their throats."
"Whose throat?" asks a very old song.
"It's not the throats that concerns me,"
says the General to his saddled horse.
"It's the antimatter?" says the horse.
"Yes," the General says, "the antimatter."

Sumo Heartthrob
Blood Dorsal
The Less Detectives
Riffer Bib
Cliff Liftoff
Lost Pauses
The Gray Flavorful
Ardor Purse
Sow Pews
Deli Berate
Pencil Hook
Carson B. Rosebush
Slap Pals
Bro Hampers
React Ion
Perjury Meg
Catty Ease
The Sot Pause
Convention Jujus
Clit Rich
Size Mile
Cleave Ito
Thunder Pungent
The Good Won't
Like Ideas
The Sneaky Camcorder
Leather Feather
The Correct Freckle
Pet Lynching
Barely Cherub

Mustard Chump
The So What Hummer
The Least Dilated
Open Nero
Glut Registers
Stud Duties
Psych Glitterati
The Sheer Reals
Forgo Toad
Bleeping Sag
Good Together
The Bad Illuminati
Gosh Hog
Hokey Bitch
Safety Restored
Roper Nomination
Oops Ear
Cob Cocks
Refuger
System Riggers
President Brown Shirt
The Lob Towards
Crying Mothers
Great Cleveland
Siphon Rightly
Terrible Terrible Crimes
Polite Dying
Darlin Nilrad
Piglet Dipshit
Inner Fails

Sepia Neat
No Good Leo
Republic Nuts
Newt Hebrew
Stited Unates
Teal Cleats
Value Lads
The Mock Tarn
Oath Moguls
The Get Rich Again
Spree Eater
Fledge Faster
Ending Wheat
Wormer Choice
Undo Dollop
Frump Disaster
Stu Dents
The Dead Inline
Gracious Prescott
Proud Dada
Glop Dignity
Teen Knife Fight
The Start Wrinkle
Feature Egypt
The Bored Audience
The Clack Act
The Empty Win
Wistful Loops
Hades Playboy
Rear Dear

The Pang Harangue
Polly Macho
Hort Shand

Acknowledgments

Thanks to the editors of the following magazines, who first published some of these poems:

Ampersand; The Awl; The Believer; Big Bell; Columbia Poetry Review; Forklift, Ohio; Masque and Spectacle; interrupture; Juked; Omniverse; Open Letters Monthly; Poet Lore; Powder Keg; Rattle; Rhino; and *Sixth Finch*

About the Author

Peter Davis's previous books of poetry are *Hitler's Mustache*, *Poetry! Poetry! Poetry!*, and *TINA*. He writes, draws, and makes music in Muncie, Indiana, where he lives with his wife and kids and teaches at Ball State University.

artisnecessary.com

www.ingramcontent.com/pod-product-compliance
Lightning Source LLC
Chambersburg PA
CBHW022102090426
42743CB00008B/689